Troubled Youth?

Young People, Violence and Disorder in Northern Ireland.

Ulf Hansson
Institute for Conflict Research

Troubled Youth?

First Published November 2005

Institute for Conflict Research
Unit 14, North City Business Centre
2 Duncairn Gardens
Belfast BT15 2GG

Tel: 028 9074 2682
Fax: 028 9035 6654
Email: info@conflictresearch.org.uk
Web: www.conflictresearch.org.uk

ISBN 0-9541898-8-4

The research was funded by the Community Relations Council through the European Special Support Programme for Peace and Reconciliation.

Produced by three creative company 028 9048 3388

Contents

1. Introduction — 3
   - Young People and the Troubles — 4
   - Violence and Disorder — 5
   - Interface Violence — 6
   - Intra Community Violence — 8
   - Summary — 9

2. Methodology — 10
   - Belfast — 10
   - Derry Londonderry — 11
   - Methods — 12
   - Participative Research — 15
   - Summary — 17

3. Young People and Violence — 18
   - Interface Violence — 18
   - City Centre Violence — 30
   - Intra Communal Violence — 32
   - Anti-Social Behaviour — 34
   - Alcohol and Violence — 39
   - Summary — 41

4. Gender and Violence — 42
   - Young Women and Violence — 53
   - Summary — 58

5. Facilities and Engagement — 59
   - Youth Facilities — 59
   - Involving Young People — 62
   - Cross-Community Work — 66
   - Summary — 69

6. Responding to Violence and Disorder — 70
   - Young People and the PSNI — 70
   - The Police and Young People — 75
   - CCTV and Violence — 82
   - Young People and the Paramilitaries — 85
   - Restorative Justice — 95
   - Summary — 97

7. Conclusions — 98

8. References — 101

9. ICR Reports — 105

1. Introduction

It was not their choice ... it was an art of defence, passed on by another generation ... I have come to the conclusion that now we are living with it so long it has become addictive. It is a continuation of something that they have learned to get a buzz from, there is excitement in it ... even a dignity and a worth in it (Protestant male).

Over recent years residents, community workers, political representatives and the police have all noted the influence of young people in sustaining tension within and between communities and participating in forms of violence and anti-social behaviour. Similarly media coverage has vividly shown that children and young people play a key role in many disturbances and outbreaks of disorder (Jarman and O'Halloran 2001). Young people themselves frequently state that they have nothing to do, which is used to explain or justify their violent behaviour. Hall (2002) in turn notes that there is a widespread perception among residents in many working class communities that young people, particularly young males, are involved in anti-social behaviour, and they are regarded as 'scum' and 'hoods'.

The aim of this report is to focus on issues of community order that are related to forms of violence, anti-social behaviour and policing. This involves looking at the relationships between communities on either side of the sectarian divide and the role of young people in defining these relationships as antagonistic, hostile and suspicious. In some areas the dominant form of violence is inter-communal, and often sectarian, which is manifest in riots at interface areas along the lines of 'defence' or 'attack'. In other areas intra-community violence dominates, where young people gang up against each other along the lines of estate versus estate or gang versus gang. Within single identity areas forms of anti-social behaviour, such as joy riding and vandalism, are often particular inter-generational problems, where young people are seen as the instigators of such activities. There is thus a legitimate focus on the specific role of children and young people in different forms of community conflict. The volatility of conflicted communities is often comprised of the activities of young petrol bombers, rock throwers and rioters, alongside a latent paramilitary capacity. Street fighting by youths is part of the armour of local communities and represents a way in which children and young people's political status within those communities can be enhanced.

However, the role of young people, especially young males, in street violence and rioting is more easily observed than understood or analysed. The role of such fighting may well be an important element in their induction and socialisation into later adult paramilitary roles. Paradoxically, however, such roles often compound generational conflict within communities, where young people are seen to be beyond the control of adults and became 'a law unto themselves' (Smyth, Hamilton and Thomson 2002). This study aims to increase understanding of the behaviour of young people who have been, or feel that they are, socially excluded within their community, and who in turn are serving to create wider feelings of disorder and disruption within these communities.

Young People and the Troubles

Some communities in Northern Ireland are characterised by residential segregation, sectarianism, intimidation, street disturbances and paramilitary activity. However, research examining the association between witnessing violence and engaging in anti-social behaviour remains distinctly limited. Miller et al (1999) and Scarpa (2001) maintain that exposure to violence during childhood can be a significant predictor of subsequent anti-social behaviour. Eitle and Turner (2002) refer to 'exposure to community violence' and claim that exposure to adversities serves to increase the risk of being involved in crime (see also Corrigan 1998). Smyth (1998) refers to a 'double penalty' where sectarian violence and disorder has exacerbated the social, psychological and environmental difficulties for people. The Troubles have had diverse effects, but it is important to stress that not all young people have had the same experiences of the conflict, the impact and their experiences of violence depend on where they live, socio-economic status and religious belonging (Boal et al 1982; Cairns 1996; Fay et al. 1997, 1999a, 1999b; Whyte 1998).

Residential segregation has been caused by and also resulted in recurrent low-level sectarian clashes and rioting, mainly in interface areas. Poole and Doherty (1996) refer to the urban areas of Belfast, Derry Londonderry and Craigavon as being the most segregated communities in Northern Ireland. A report by the Northern Ireland Housing Executive (1999) indicated that 98% of its stock in Belfast and 71% of the stock in Northern Ireland is in segregated areas. Connolly and McGinn (1999) highlighted how children as young as three years of age were able to identify, and also attribute positive and negative characteristics to, Catholics or Protestants. Kelly (2002) refers to the role played by parents in influencing children's attitudes to sectarianism and the promotion of negative views of people from other communities and notes that in some cases parents encouraged participation in violent behaviour, such as rioting. The Troubles have helped not only to create feelings of suspicion and fear between the two main communities, but also a sense of grievance and victimhood. This is often based on real wrongs and injustice, and has been referred to as a 'grievance culture' where children grow up 'inheriting these grievances and learn that, from a very early age, wrongs have been done to them or their kith and kin (Smyth and Scott 2000). Children and young people can thus be seen as both victims and perpetrators of violence.

Statistical evidence from the Cost of the Troubles Study (Fay et al. 1999b) revealed that young people were at the highest risk of being killed, with almost 26% of all victims being aged 21 or less. In 30 years of conflict, 557 young people under the age of 20 have been killed and it is estimated that 32% of young people aged 14-18 years of age have witnessed someone being killed or seriously injured. Previous research (Smyth 1998) established that deaths in Northern Ireland were concentrated in a relatively small area, particularly in urban areas, mainly North and West Belfast and Derry Londonderry and these areas had also experienced 58% of all deaths of those under the age of 18. Smyth concludes that:

What emerges from this is that certain sub-groups of children and young people are identified as being particularly at risk of becoming victims (or perpetrators) of violent acts (Smyth 1998: 47).

Violence and Disorder

Sectarian clashes are not new to Northern Ireland, but since the ceasefires in 1994 there has been a sustained if erratic backdrop of violence, in which young people play a prominent role. According to McEvoy-Levy (2001) young people's perceptions of violence are shaped by local history, by parental and community influence, and by direct experiences of violence. Despite the peace process, violence remains an immediate experience (and memory) for many young people and the association of religious identification with the threat of violence is strong. Many young people grow up in polarised communities with their own specific identities and culture, making it difficult for them to build friendships with those from other traditions.

Areas severely affected by the Troubles have experienced high levels of paramilitary and security force activity. Smyth, Hamilton, and Thomson (2002:18) refer to young people who have:

Spent all their lives including formative years within an ideology that legitimises the use of violence in the pursuit of certain political aims.

Aspects of this 'culture of violence' have subsequently passed into local communities and have become normalised (Harland 2001). In order to survive the violence and brutality of the Troubles, many people, including children and young people, have become socialised and habituated to violence. At times they may minimise violence, which has enabled them to survive psychologically (Smyth and Scott 2000).

Jarman (2002) provides a framework of background issues that impact on violence, such as parades, policing, territoriality and segregation. He writes of a culture which 'celebrate and commemorate acts of violence' and that this creates an 'ideological packaging which seems to justify and rationalise acts of violence'. Jarman also suggests that the reasons for violence and anti-social behaviour are multi-layered, although there is a tendency, perhaps too readily, to refer to lack of resources, opportunities and segregation. McEvoy-Levy (2001) feels that young people continue to experience and produce violence at the micro level, this violence comes in various forms: sectarian assaults, interface street fighting, mass protests or rioting at marches. All of these incidents hold the potential for escalation and legitimise the maintenance of exclusive sectarian communities for reasons of protection.

Interface Violence

An interface has been described as 'the common boundary between a predominantly Protestant/Unionist area and a predominantly Catholic/Nationalist area', while an interface community is the residential population that lives alongside an interface (Jarman 2002: 21). Previous research has established that various forms of anti-social behaviour and violence have particularly affected interface areas. However, Belfast Interface Project (1998: 8) states that:

Violence is largely perpetuated from each interface's 'hinterland' community, while the interface community serves as a 'human shield' and front line of defence for that hinterland.

The people living on the interface therefore tend to be the receivers of violence more than perpetrators (Jarman and O'Halloran 2000, 2001). This is supported by a report by Woodvale Resource Centre (1998), where the majority of the respondents said they had taken part in stone throwing along the peace-line, but the majority of young people involved in the interface violence did not live in the immediate area. Interviewees referred to friends from outside 'joining in', in order to defend the area. Respondents said that this gave them 'a feeling of common purpose'. The interface areas also tend to be popular places for young people to 'hang out', even though these areas often do not have youth clubs or facilities, but mean young people can be out of sight of adults (Woodvale Resource Centre 1998). Jarman and O'Halloran (2001:3) discuss the role of young people in 'recreational rioting', which they describe as:

Another form of anti-social behaviour, which is emerging as a persistent problem as Northern Ireland struggles to establish itself as a peaceful democratic society. However, these forms of recreational rioting can all too easily feed into more inclusive forms of sectarian violence.

Other research identified similar issues in which respondents saw violence and vandalism as 'something exciting' and 'fun' in situations otherwise characterised by boredom and apathy (Hall 1999; Todd 2002). At the same time the young people interviewed were aware of the risks involved and this, to a certain extent, 'made for more excitement'.

Previous research has also shown that adults in the community may allow the problem to build up and the violence to continue so that they can show their power and authority by stopping it when the time is right. This type of orchestrated violence can often take place at an interface, while armed paramilitary groupings may also be behind premeditated forms of violence. The attitude of adults in encouraging such behaviour one minute and condemning it the next sends conflicting and confusing messages to young people and also helps to undermine any sense of adult authority (Smyth 2001).

Disorder and violence can therefore be seen as acceptable or normal, as young people receive 'mixed signals' from the adult community. Jarman and O'Halloran (2001) write that marches are often excuses for rioting or violence, but violence may also be associated with a variety of events as tension is ignited by a range of sporting, cultural or political activities. This 'culture of violence' also involves a legacy of celebrating and commemorating acts of violence and a belief that violence has been a necessary and useful means of promoting and defending political ambitions (Jarman 2004).

Intra-Community Violence

Troubles-related violence still has an impact in Northern Ireland through fear, suspicion and the limited interaction between the two main communities, but there is also a need to acknowledge the problem of violence within communities. Non-sectarian violence, such as city-centre violence and attacks outside pubs and clubs, appear to be increasing. Some have referred to a shifting balance between sectarian violence and non-sectarian violence (McGrellis 2004), with violence between young men also likely to occur among those from neighbouring communities of the same religious background. Some young men feel that violence is a natural feature of male youth culture and is thus deemed 'inescapable' (Harland 2001; Reilly, Muldoon and Byrne 2004). Violence is seen as an expression of young men's hopelessness, frustration, isolation, boredom and energy, but also plays a role in maintaining status and building a reputation. Young men describe themselves as living in a culture of violence, where violence is the norm for settling problems. This is a shared reality for both Protestants and Catholics (Reilly, Muldoon and Byrne 2004).

Some recognition of this culture of violence encompassing young people has become evident through the contemporary debate on anti-social behaviour. In many of the areas involved in the research one of the major concerns is the 'apparent' rise in forms of anti-social behaviour and low-level violence and disorder. This current disorder is largely seen as being caused by young people. A survey by the Northern Ireland Policing Board indicated that 'young people causing a nuisance' was the third most significant problem after domestic burglary and underage drinking across Northern Ireland (Northern Ireland Policing Board 2004:3-4) and many police command units cite young people as the major source of complaints. The issue of problematic young people has thus become a major feature on the policy agenda in Britain and Ireland. In England and Wales anti-social behaviour was highlighted as a problem through the Crime and Disorder Act (1998) and the Anti-Social Behaviour Act (1999) and in August 2004, Security Minister John Spellar in turn introduced Anti-Social Behaviour Orders in Northern Ireland. Thus while some of the forms of violence involving young people that we explore are largely specific to Northern Ireland, the category of problematic and disorderly youths has become a much more widely cited concern.

Summary

The involvement of young people in various forms of violence and public disorder has been highlighted in a range of research in recent years. Much of this work has focused on one specific type or category violence, but what is becoming increasingly evident is that the boundaries separating the different types of violence are very porous. Approaches that help to rationalise or explain disorder at interfaces are thus relevant to understanding city centre disorder and anti-social behaviour. This report aims to look at the attitudes of young people to a variety of forms of public disorder and violence in order to better understand the persistent problems being experienced in many areas across Northern Ireland.

2. Methodology

For the research it was necessary to identify areas that have experienced different intensities of violence, disorder and anti-social behaviour. Two main localities were chosen as the focus of the research, North Belfast and Derry Londonderry, and a number of smaller areas in each city were targeted for more detailed work. It is important here to make the point that these areas are not assumed to be representative of Northern Ireland as a whole; rather the different areas provide complementary insights into the attitudes and experiences of young people, as well as older members of the community, living in areas affected by violence and anti-social behaviour.

Belfast

The Troubles have been overwhelmingly concentrated in Belfast: over 40% of deaths occurred within the city, although it contains only 20% of the regional population. Certain kinds of violence were even more concentrated, with almost half of all sectarian deaths occurring in Belfast. The degree of spatial segmentation represented by peace-lines and residential segregation is much greater than in other areas of Northern Ireland. North Belfast has a large number of interfaces and has become associated with high levels of political tension, violence and socio-economic deprivation. The area can be divided into three or four relatively large and connected areas of loyalist or nationalist estates and streets. The Shore Road is a continuous area of Protestant communities from Tiger's Bay to Graymount, while there is a larger Protestant area in North and West Belfast that includes the Greater Shankill and Ballysillan areas. The large nationalist zones are from Ardoyne to the New Lodge along the Cliftonville Road and along the Antrim Road from New Lodge to Fortwilliam. There are also a number of relatively isolated areas in which the people can feel more vulnerable at times of tension. For this project, research was carried out in five interface areas: New Lodge, Newington, and Tiger's Bay in the inner city and White City and Whitewell in outer North Belfast. The sixth area, Sunningdale, which is part of Ballysillan, has no interface.

New Lodge-Newington-Tiger's Bay: According to the most recent Census, the New Lodge area has a population of 5,224, which is 97% Catholic. Young people under the age of 20 make up 34% of the population (NISRA 2001). New Lodge experiences both economic and social deprivation and is bounded by a 'peace-line' along Duncairn Gardens, which faces Tiger's Bay. New Lodge merges into Newington along the Antrim Road, an area which also includes Alexandra Park and the interface on Limestone Road with Tiger's Bay. Tiger's Bay falls under the Duncairn Ward and is a predominantly Protestant area, albeit dwindling. The Census shows the ward having a 2% Catholic population and 70% Protestant. The Limestone Road interface between Tiger's Bay and Newington has seen severe violence in the form of street fighting and riots in recent years.

Whitewell-White City: The Whitewell area encompasses the Whitewell Road, White City and Serpentine Gardens. Until 1996 the two areas co-existed relatively peacefully, but recurrent violence since that year led to the construction of a barrier, almost 200 metres long and up to 15 metres high, between the two communities in 1999. As well as the divisions between the predominantly Catholic Whitewell and Protestant White City, there are several other interfaces between the Throne area, Arthur's Bridge, Longlands, Rathcoole, Bawnmore and Graymount in what has become a complex mosaic of intersecting communities.

Sunningdale: The Sunningdale area is bordered by Ballysillan Road to the north and Cavehill Road to the east. The 2001 Census estimates the population to be 1,224. There is no overt interface in the area but the young people expressed concerns about the junction between Cavehill Road and North Circular Road, while adults have identified anti-social behaviour, crime and young people congregating in the nearby Cavehill Country Park as problem issues.

Derry Londonderry

Residential segregation in Derry Londonderry has increased over recent years and the city is now largely divided by the River Foyle, with a Catholic majority on the City-side and a Protestant majority on the Waterside. Tensions over parades have been reduced and sectarian violence is now contained to a limited number of areas of the city. However, in contrast to Belfast, the central area of the city has become an often dangerous place to be late at night as a result of the presence of rival gangs of youths who, although from the same community, regard each other with hostility and antagonism. City centre violence has been a serious problem leading to demands for an increased police presence and the installation of a CCTV system to monitor the violence. Three areas were selected for research in Derry Londonderry, the main interface communities of the Fountain and the Bogside, and the Galliagh estate in Shantallow.

The Fountain-Bogside: This interface, mainly along Bishop Street, has seen regular incidents involving young people throwing petrol and paint bombs from either side. The Fountain is a Protestant area situated within the Diamond Ward on the west bank of the city, with housing predominantly owned by the Housing Executive. The population is small, estimated to be 300, and has been declining over recent years. The Fountain faces the city walls and Bishop Street in the north and in the south borders Abercorn Road and the Craigavon Bridge. Bishop Street and Abercorn Road have had extended fencing erected. The predominately Catholic Bogside area is in the Westland and Brandywell electoral wards. The TRIAX Taskforce report (2003) estimated the population at 5,098, with 45% being under the age of 16.

Galliagh: is a predominately Catholic estate. It is part of the Greater Shantallow Area some five miles from the city centre. The Greater Shantallow Area has a population of approximately 30,000 people, 38% of the total population of the Derry City Council area. The Galliagh estate was built in the late 1970's and has a population of approximately 1,500. The Community Safety Survey (NIACRO 2001) estimated that 1,400 of the households in Galliagh were on housing benefits and that 40% of primary and secondary school children received free school meals.

Methods

The research included both qualitative and quantitative methods including participant observation, individual interviews, focus groups, reviews of local newspapers and some survey work in each of the two main areas.

Participant Observation: Focus groups alone were felt not to be adequate to elicit the information and insights necessary to understand the views of young people. A more participatory approach was developed which involved attending events in the individual areas and meeting with young people and youth workers outside of a formal research setting. The researcher focused on building relationships with adults and young people in each of the locations before formal research work was carried out. This involved, for example, meeting young people at places where they 'hung out' or when there was a communal event in the area, such as a parade or a bonfire, often together with representatives from the community.

Interviews: Youth workers and leaders provided invaluable help and assistance with the fieldwork, but also acted as gatekeepers in accessing groups of young people. Interviews were conducted with youth and community workers, representatives from youth organisations, members of educational, legal and policing authorities and local residents. Interviewees were contacted through community centres and youth clubs and were given the opportunity to ask questions and highlight issues of importance. These interviews also helped to put the research within a context.

Paper Review: Articles relating to young people along with incidents of violent behaviour in the community were collected from the press covering both cities. Several themes emerged from the articles, which highlighted issues relating to young people, and these were then discussed in the interviews.

Focus Groups: A variety of themes were used to guide the discussions. The use of focus groups enabled the researcher to more formally record opinions and attitudes and allowed issues raised in other areas of research to be further explored. The following themes were used to guide the focus groups: perception of the area in which they lived: number of clubs, type of clubs, things to do in the area. This also involved cultural activities, such as bonfires; experiences and attitudes towards cross-community work, particularly on the interface areas; access to pubs, clubs and off-licenses and attitudes to alcohol; interface issues, including safety, accessing facilities and amenities; experiences of, and involvement in, various forms of violence and anti-social behaviour; the role of paramilitaries, CCTV and general relationship with the police. The focus group discussions with the young people highlighted similar issues in each area and indicated that all young people face the same kind of problems.

Whenever possible the focus groups were tape-recorded, however on some occasions the participants did not want the discussion recorded. In these situations the groups allowed the researcher to take notes. In most cases the discussions lasted between 45 and 90 minutes, and in some cases groups met on more than one occasion. When interviewing young people, particularly those under the age of 18, consent forms were used to ensure that all participants fully understood the nature of the research. Participants in focus groups were accessed through youth clubs or community programmes. In almost all of the focus groups, the youth worker/leader remained present. On occasion this hindered discussions or steered them in a certain direction, but at times their presence stimulated discussion. Throughout the research process the researcher aimed to facilitate the focus groups in the areas and accommodate the young people.

A total of 10 formal focus groups were held with 132 participants (67 males and 65 females) in six groups in North Belfast and four in Derry Londonderry (Table 1). Most young people were aged between 14 and 17, of which some had been involved in crime and some having convictions. These young people tend to have low self-esteem, poor communication skills, little or no academic achievement and were either involved in antisocial or criminally motivated behaviour or have the potential to become involved. Socially excluded young people were also selected to take part. One group involved young men who have been excluded from their communities.

Table 1. Locations and participants for focus groups

Area	Total	Gender	Age	Community Background
Fountain	9	5 Male 4 Female	1x15,2 x 16, 1x17,1x18 2 x 18,1x16,1x17	Protestant
Galliagh	9	6 Male 3 Female	5x18 and 1x21 1x15,1x16,1x17	Catholic
Ballysillan	7	7 Female	1x11,3x13, 2x15, 1x16	Protestant
Bogside	12	6 Male 6 Female	1x12,1x15,3 x 16,1x18 3x14,3x16	Catholic
Derry	23	13 Male 10 Female	2x14,1x15,2x16,3x17, 1x18, 1x20, 2x21,1x22 5x17, 2x16, 1x20, 1x21, 1x25	Mixed
New Lodge	9	9 Male	2x12,1x13,2x14,2x15, 2x16	Catholic
Tigers Bay/ Shore Road	20	10 Male 10 Female	1x14, 6x 12-14, 1x23,2x18 3x15, 2x18, 5x12-14	Protestant
White City	7	5 Female 2 Male	3x13, 2 x14 1x12, 1x13	Protestant
Whitewell	9	5 Female 4 Male	2x14,2x16,1x17 4x16	Catholic
Sunningdale	13	6 Female 7 Male	3x14,1x15, 2x16 7x16+	Protestant
Newington	14	5 Male 9 Female	1x15,1x16,2x17,1x18 4x14,5x15	Catholic
Total	132	67 Male 65 Female		

Limitations on Participation: Some groups who were approached were unwilling to participate in the research, either because they perceived the research to be controversial or too personal, or because they felt they had been over researched. It also proved difficult to access young people from older age groups (20+) and the emphasis therefore shifted to younger participants. A particular barrier to participation was the issue of 'research fatigue', which was alluded to by both young people and adults. There was a strong sense among some groups that sufficient research had already taken place and, significantly, that little practical outcome had resulted from this. At the same time, 'research fatigue' had to be balanced with a consideration of how many young people have participated directly in any research and how many of them have had the opportunity to articulate their experiences.

To ensure that the participants felt a degree of ownership over the research, it was agreed that workshops would be held with participants in each of the areas before any publication of the research. This would enable participants and communities to comment on the research. In the report back sessions the various groups felt the research adequately highlighted their situation and their experiences. There was also a sense among young people, particularly on the interfaces, that the findings from the neighbouring areas were of particular interest. In some cases groups expressed surprise when hearing of the similarities and also the issues young people dealt with.

Confidentiality and Sensitivity: it was also pertinent to ensure that information and material would not be disclosed in a way that would reveal the identity of the participants. The researcher therefore had to reassure young people of the independence and confidentiality of the research. In addition to confidentiality, there was also an awareness of the sensitivity of the subject and some activities, such as interface violence and underage drinking. In some cases young people felt they were singled out and that the activities they were involved in would get unwanted attention from the community and/or the police.

Participative Research

As part of the process of engaging with young people and identifying key issues in each of the areas, ICR made contact with a variety of organisations working with young people. These contacts in turn identified a range of concerns that had been raised about the role of research in some communities and in particular the frequency with which some communities and some organisations had become the subjects of the research process, and through which knowledge and information was taken from an area, but little was returned. This led to discussions about developing a more interactive and reciprocal approach to the overall research project and this in turn led to the practical development of a number of distinct research projects which, while falling within the broad theme of the main project, were distinct in and of themselves.

In each case the specific subject of the research project was determined by the local group and ICR provided advice, support and training to community based organisations to enable them to undertake research which fed into the aims and objectives of the group. Through this process, ICR were able to build more open and constructive relationships with a number of key organisations working with issues related to young people and worked with the groups to produce independent reports of the research, which were utilised by the group to develop their future practice (Byrne, Hansson and Jarman 2005). ICR were also able to draw on the research findings for this report.

To date eight community research projects have been developed through this process. These have included five projects in Belfast: in Lower North Belfast (young people's involvement in electoral politics), Sunningdale (crime and anti-social behaviour), Ballysillan (the role of the churches in community activity), New Lodge (young women and violence) and Whitewell (a community audit) and two projects in Galliagh on young people's experiences of violence, and understandings of the concept of anti-social behaviour. A further project on young people's experiences of sectarianism was conducted with the YMCA in Larne. The following offers a brief description of the three projects developed as part of the young people and violence project.

ICR worked with Off the Streets Youth Initiative in Galliagh to design and conduct a survey among pupils at St Brigid's College in Galliagh. A total of 417 pupils from the college completed the survey, which explored understandings and experiences of violence and conflict in the area. The questionnaire also covered issues relating to family life, facilities and amenities in the area and involvement in anti-social behaviour. The questionnaire highlighted the extent of young people's involvement in various forms of anti-social behaviour. This survey helped to inform the research about young people's attitudes in the area and added to the qualitative findings. The research report was written up in conjunction with staff at Off the Streets and launched at a public seminar in Galliagh in December 2004 (Off the Streets et al 2004). It is available online at www.conflictresearch.org.uk. The report is being used by Off the Streets to inform its future practical work, its strategic focus and its relationships with other agencies in the area. ICR are also supporting Off the Streets in further research in the area.

ICR worked with North Belfast Alternatives and LINC Resource Centre to develop a project in the Sunningdale area to explore local understandings and concerns about levels of crime and anti-social behaviour and the role of the police in dealing with these issues. This project involved working with a group of young people to design a questionnaire and survey local residents and young people about their differing perceptions. The young people also held discussions with local politicians, with the PSNI and with local young people, which were fed into the final report. The report was launched at a public event in Sunningdale and has been used by North Belfast Alternatives in developing its future activities (Mourlon and Hansson 2004). The report is also available on the ICR website at www.conflictresearch.org.uk.

The third project involved working with staff and young women at the Artillery Youth Club in the New Lodge to develop a project on the perceptions and experiences of young women in the Greater New Lodge area to various forms of violence. This project grew out of a training programme being run through the youth club for young women and is designed to feed into a further stage of working with young women in the area. The research report will be available at www.conflictresearch.org.uk when it is fully finalised.

Summary

The research project on young people and violence has involved a diverse methodology, which included participant observation, interviews, focus groups, informal discussions, surveys and an innovative form of participative action research, and which were spread over a variety of distinct areas in both Belfast and Derry Londonderry.

The next chapter of the report explores the young people's views, experiences and understandings of various forms of violence in their lives. This is followed by a chapter focusing on the gendered aspects of violence and the specific perceptions of young women in relation to this issue. The report then continues with a chapter that focuses on the issue of the provision of youth facilities and activities and finally a chapter on young people's perceptions of the main structures of adult authority.

3. Young People and Violence

This section of the study explores how young people from a number of communities across Northern Ireland experience, understand and respond to different forms of violence. The focus of the research is on specific forms of public violence and includes violence around interface areas and in city centres, as well as forms of violence and anti-social behaviour that takes place within predominately single identity communities. Interface violence is a common feature of life for many parts of North Belfast and between the Fountain and Bogside areas of Derry Londonderry. City centre violence has also emerged as a persistent problem in Derry Londonderry, but appears to have been less of an issue for the young people we interviewed in North Belfast. Violence within communities emerged as a particular concern in the Galliagh estate in Derry Londonderry, but again it was difficult to confirm that this problem existed on the same scale in the communities we researched in North Belfast. Finally, discussions on and about the concept of anti-social behaviour identified a variety of often low-level activities, many of which have in the past been categorised as 'youths causing annoyance', as a growing problem in many areas.

Interface Violence

In Derry Londonderry, the part of the Fountain estate facing onto Bishop Street is the area where most interface violence in the city occurs. This violence mainly involves various types of missiles, including bottles, stones, petrol bombs and blast bombs, being thrown over the interface barrier either into or from the Fountain. During 2003 reports of sectarian incidents around the interface began to appear in the local media in March and carried on through the spring and into July. This pattern, by which violence begins around Easter and continues through into summer, is familiar from other interface areas in Northern Ireland (Jarman 1997, Byrne 2005). In most cases, the riots and disturbances resulted from attacks on the Fountain estate, when the police responded they would be confronted by groups of young people, sometimes from a Republican and sometimes a Loyalist background, who then turned on the police. One of the worst incidents in 2003 occurred on 2 July, when the PSNI were attacked by up to 12 petrol bombs thrown from the Bishop Street area. What made this particular incident noteworthy is that some of the petrol bombs contained sugar, which transformed the flames into a substance similar to napalm. A sixteen-year-old youth was subsequently charged in connection with these events (*Belfast Telegraph* 3 July 2003, *Derry Journal* 4 July 2003, *Belfast Telegraph* 8 July 2003).

The PSNI recorded a total of 60 incidents at Bishop Street between April 2003 and January 2004 (Table 2). Apart from petrol bombing incidents and hoax bombs, the category of 'disturbances' includes paint bombing, stone throwing, firing of fireworks, youth causing annoyance and disorderly arrests. Although violence around the Bishop Street interface is a persistent problem, it is worth noting that the number of interface incidents declined during the summer, the main part of the marching season. Furthermore, the police also noted that serious incidents on the interface fell by some 81% compared to the previous year.

Table 2. Disturbances at Bishop Street interface April 2003 to January 2004

Incident	April	May	June	July	August	Sept/Jan	Total
Petrol bomb	2	0	1	4	2	8	17
Hoax bomb	0	1	3	0	0	2	6
Disturbances	5	5	4	3	1	10	28
Criminal damage	5	2	1	1	0	0	9
Total	12	8	9	8	3	20	60

Source: PSNI Foyle DCU.

North Belfast has suffered from extensive violence at numerous interfaces since serious violence erupted in the summer of 1996 (Jarman 2002). Each year the tension increases in the numerous interfaces across the area in response to various contentious parades, while the most sustained period of violence occurred at the time of the Holy Cross dispute in 2001 (Cadwallader 2004). However the overall number of incidents has been considerably reduced since 2002, as can be seen from statistics from the three interface areas studied in North Belfast: Tiger's Bay-New Lodge (Table 3), Tiger's Bay-Newington (Table 4) and Whitewell-White City (Table 5). The reduction in the number of incidents appears to have been due to a combination of factors including the work done by community activists, changes in policing, the introduction of CCTV cameras in many locations, and a reorientation of the approach of the UDA to interface violence in the area

Table 3. Disturbances between New Lodge and Tigers Bay 2002 to 2005

Incident	2002/2003	2003/2004	2004/2005
Riot	0	1	0
Disturbance	11	16	1
Petrol Bomb	4	0	0
Criminal damage	34	15	8
Assault	19	4	9
Intimidation	1	1	0
Total	69	37	18

Source: PSNI North Belfast DCU

Table 4. Disturbances between Newington and Tigers Bay 2002 to 2005

Incident	2002/2003	2003/2004	2004/2005
Riot	0	0	0
Disturbance	15	25	3
Petrol Bomb	2	0	0
Criminal damage	50	10	12
Assault	30	11	8
Intimidation	5	5	2
Total	102	51	25

Source: PSNI North Belfast DCU

Table 5. Disturbances in Whitewell - White City area 2002 to 2005

Incident	2002/2003	2003/2004	2004/2005
Riot	0	0	2
Disturbance	16	41	18
Petrol Bomb	1	0	1
Criminal damage	100	45	38
Assault	33	20	17
Intimidation	13	7	11
Total	163	113	87

Source: PSNI North Belfast DCU

Young People and Interface Violence

Over the course of numerous conversations and interviews it was possible to explore the views of young people towards interface violence. One of the key issues was to identify how the young people felt the fighting started at interfaces. Many of them found it hard to associate attacks with any particular event or time of day, though often references would be made to particular parades or to results of football matches – often the old-firm games between Rangers and Celtic caused violence to start. However, frequently the violence appeared to erupt from very little except an exchange of verbal abuse:

There will be slabbering ... and then its starts (Catholic male).

In some cases the young people referred to the unpredictability of attacks or interaction on the interface:

You can hardly say, it just kicks off ... insults fly...and then bricks and bottles are thrown ... or sometimes things can happen just out of the blue (Protestant Male).

Many of the young people said that they could not see the point of these incidents, indeed as one young interviewee stated:

It is actually stupid; it is not about religion (Protestant Female).

Numerous discussions involved exploring whether one side had more responsibility than the other and whether it was Protestants or Catholics that instigated the violence, but both sides accepted some responsibility:

You can't say it is always the Catholics ... see if there is a car coming up ... and by the bridge, we would brick it or something ... or shout. Say we saw somebody walking up ... we would run after them ... and then older ones would join...and then them ones would come up and then they all start fighting (Protestant female).

Members of the younger age group said that it often tended to be 'really young kids' who started the trouble by throwing stones, and then older ones would join in. Many young people agreed that young people were in the forefront of trouble breaking out and very much involved in the violence. Young people stated that they felt they were often encouraged to play an active role in interface violence and therefore only did what they were encouraged to do. However, at the same time the presence of young people in these incidents provoked strong reactions from some of the participants and the young people themselves felt that even if young people did not start the violence, very often they were left to take the blame from the wider community, including the paramilitaries:

See if there is a riot ... we tend to be in the front-line and we will be the ones getting caught ... its all kids ... we will all be caught (Protestant male).

Interestingly enough, while the research was in progress the Real IRA called on young people to stop attacking the Fountain, and at the same time defended 'the right of anyone to attack the forces of British occupation' (*Derry Journal* 17 February 2004). While such statements may try to reduce some tensions between communities, they also assert that some forms of violence are still considered to be acceptable and legitimate.

Some of the young people argued that the violence was in many ways part of a 'tit for tat' culture, in which attacks across an interface were carried out in response to previous violence from the other side, or even violence in other towns. A group of young males, claiming to be members of Bogside Republican Youth (a group of young unaffiliated republicans), said that attacks on Protestants in the Fountain only took place if Catholic areas like the Short Strand in Belfast, were targeted. Some young people in the Bogside felt that this was perhaps the only way that they could *'get their point across'*. In some cases interviewees in both Protestant and Catholic areas saw themselves as 'defenders' of their area, while the means of providing defence of their community could also extend to attacking the neighbouring area. At the time of the research, the Fountain estate suffered a number of petrol and paint bomb attacks and young men in the area felt that there was a need to be more pro-active:

Ay, that's the only way to sort it out like ... with bottles, stones ... attacks on houses in the Bogside, just to get them to stop (Protestant males).

This emphasis on the need to defend their area was heightened by the fact that the Fountain was the last Protestant enclave on the west bank of the town. Some of the young people thus argued that it was time to take a stand and to defend the area, before it was too late.

In other locations acts of violence were considered to be a justified reaction or an appropriate response to such events as parades and to the presence of bonfires. The participants' views on parades and sectarian displays were clearly divided and it was difficult to establish any sense of a middle ground. One group of young Catholic men in North Belfast felt that all parades were wrong and therefore their violent actions against parades were justified, while in other cases young people agreed that throwing stones at a march was an acceptable means of showing their opposition to the event. For young Protestants, in contrast, violence towards parades in any location merely hardened their resolve in support of parades in general.

The involvement of young people in interface violence can perhaps best be described as occurring through the actions of young males acting in rather loosely formed groups. Such actions are designed to focus on defending their own territory from neighbouring areas, even if the best form of defence is attack. However, the young men do not act as systematically organised units and, although the violence is sometimes encouraged by adults within their community, they are not under formal paramilitary control.

The belief in the need to be actively involved in physically defending their area or their culture was particularly strong among the young men, who in interviews and focus groups referred to their experiences on the interface and their involvement in violence and disorder. In contrast although young women might refer to being present at the time of a riot, they usually denied any active involvement. In some instances however, the young women referred to throwing stones at vehicles leaving a neighbouring estate, but they rarely admitted any involvement in riots or fighting on the interface. The specific experiences of young women towards various forms of violence will be considered in more detail in Chapter 4.

Boredom and Excitement

The young people in both cities made numerous references to their participation in interface violence as being an exciting activity and a change from the boredom of daily routines. This has already been acknowledged to the extent that much of the recurrent interface violence is commonly referred to as 'recreational rioting'. In some cases the young people referred to the rioting as being a *'good buzz'* or *'good craic'*. Similarly a group of young people in the Bogside discussing interface violence and the attraction it had for young people described it as *'good watching'*, thus indicating that it can be an enjoyable spectacle as much as a participatory activity. Riots were seen by some of the young people as providing *'entertainment'* or more simply as *'something to do'*. Many of the young people identified rioting as one way to relieve the boredom:

Ay (laughter) ... *boredom, that is what it is...boredom* (Protestant males).

Indeed young people in Tiger's Bay felt that most of the violence was now more likely to be due to boredom than being related to any local or national political situation. This was particularly the case during the summer months, as it provided an alternative to the boredom of the long holidays. Some young people, however, did not agree that rioting was good craic and were more aware of the possible implications of interface violence:

It is not fun ... some of them can really hurt (Protestant female).

Many of the young people did refer to the risks involved in rioting and said that sometimes they were scared when rioting broke out in their area, thus highlighting that not all young people found these situations to be entertainment. Even some of those young people who had been involved in a riot described the feeling of fear that they felt when violence broke out:

It was scary, that was the scariest thing ever ... there was no fence, there was street to street violence ... they were charging up the street ... everybody was involved in the violence ... mostly fists ... stones and bottles and everything (Protestant male).

The incident being described had taken place some two years previously, but was referred to extensively among the group of young men in the area. However, although many of the young males agreed that being involved in riots and public disorder could be scary, others said that this was not something you thought about much:

You just forget about it, there is a new one the day after (Catholic male).

When asked whether or not they felt that peer-pressure to 'join in' played a role in them becoming involved in violence on the interface there was a mixed response. The young people in the Bogside felt that peer pressure was not a factor, however some of them did acknowledge that members of the younger age groups could be under more pressure to join in and become involved, and thus be *'like everyone else'*.

It was not possible to ascertain if there was any more deliberate or considered rationale to the violence among young people. In some cases the young people regarded interface violence or attacks on the neighbouring areas and on police and army vehicles as part of a continued struggle, but others were less convinced. One young woman felt that when young people became involved in street violence they were simply *'mimicking'* their parents, but she believed that they had no idea why violence took place in the first place. In some cases it was clear that adults within their communities had influenced the arguments used by young people in relation to rioting. Some of the participants talked about the rioting in North Belfast in 1996 and 1997, but they could not really put these riots in to any context, and they were not really aware of what had actually happened to spark the violence in the first place. Most worryingly the violence seems to have become such a feature of 'normal' life that it had become a part of the local tradition, something which had always been done and which will therefore inevitably continue. As one young woman put it:

It is part of a tradition, a culture (Catholic female).

Weapons

If some young people regarded interface violence as largely spontaneous, a means of relieving boredom and having fun, others clearly regarded it as a more serious and planned activity. In some areas, the riots were described as little more than regular 'fist-fights' among the older participants, while any weapons that might be used were likely to be little more than stones, bricks or bottles, that happened to be handy, and which were more likely to be thrown by younger participants. However, some of the young people interviewed for this research talked about the different types of weapons that might be used during violent incidents at interfaces. They discussed the use of ball bearings, paint bombs, blast bombs and coffee-jar bombs, all of which might be thrown at both individuals and houses. The young men from Bogside Republican Youth talked of using petrol bombs, paint bombs and fireworks during their attacks. Two of the members of the BRY also referred to making petrol bombs and adding sugar to the mix to create an effect like napalm. This group was also perhaps the most radical of the groups in the research and they would refer to their attacks on neighbouring areas and police vehicles in military terms.

The young people in North Belfast were also aware of a wide variety of weapons that might be available to and used by young people in both Catholic and Protestant areas. There was concern among some young Catholics that people on the other side had a wider range of more violent weapons than they did and were prepared to use more lethal force if necessary:

Bricks and stones, that's what we are fighting with … they fight with f-ing pipe-bombs and anything like (Catholic male).

However, similar comments were made among young Protestants in the Tiger's Bay area about their counterparts on the Catholic side. This suggests that on both sides there was a feeling that people in the other community were prepared to use more violent weapons and be more aggressive than people on *'our side'*.

Adults and Community Workers

We have already hinted at the ambivalence that young people feel towards the role of adults in relation to interface violence and some were openly critical of the attitudes and behaviour of some adults. One young woman in Tiger's Bay said that she felt that most adults in the area did little to assist in preventing interface violence, although she did acknowledge the role played by local church groups in trying to calm things down along the interface. Many of the young people felt that adults were in no position to be critical of their actions as they were likely to have been involved in such activities themselves in the past. Some of the respondents noted that while many parents often tried to prevent their own children becoming involved in violence, other adults may well be encouraging young people to get involved in forms of disorder. Some young people felt that adults could and should do more:

If they are not encouraging them, they are certainly not stopping them (Protestant female).

One youth worker in the Bogside discussed how difficult it was working in the area and trying to prevent young people from becoming involved in the interface violence:

It has been one of the most difficult tasks, because of the abuse I have taken from young people (Catholic youth worker).

This youth worker had tried on several occasions to negotiate with young people to get them to stay away from the interface and get involved in alternative activities, but with mixed success. He had organised activities, such as trips to Belfast, at the time of potential disturbances linked to parades in Derry. In some instances however, the young people were not interested in such trips and instead seemed intent on causing havoc on the interface.

Among the youth workers and adults interviewed for the research, there was a sense of inevitability in the young people's involvement in interface violence. There was also a belief that rioting had become a multi-generational activity and that the young people did not get involved out of any real sense of choice:

It was not their choice ... it was an art of defence, passed on by another generation ... I have come to the conclusion that now we are living with it so long it has become addictive. It is a continuation of something that they have learned to get a buzz from, there is excitement in it ... even a dignity and a worth in it (Protestant male).

Another community worker, from the Fountain, said that the situation around the interface was becoming an increasing problem and adults had a responsibility to be more active and try to prevent the problems from escalating still further. He said that on occasions they had to hold young people back from becoming involved in violence, while at the same time trying to defuse a situation at the interface. He also noted that the community workers often had difficulty trying to convince the young people that it was not their job to defend their area or respond to attacks:

What we are trying to do is show them that by stepping back and let the police go and sort it out, they [the young people] don't have to get in bother, the police is getting paid to do that, let the police go and do that. Keep them [young people] back let them occupy their minds somewhere else (Protestant male).

A similar picture emerged in conversations with adults and community workers in North Belfast, who referred to difficulties in controlling interface violence. One youth worker described herself as being 'redundant' once any interface violence started:

The paramilitaries take over and we are asked to step aside (Protestant youth worker).

There was thus a resigned acknowledgement among many adults in the various areas that once violence had started it was very difficult trying to prevent young people from joining in such activities. Numerous schemes had been established to attract young people away from the interfaces, and these were recognised by both youth and community workers to be relatively successful. However, people also acknowledged that the available funding was limited and they would always struggle to provide enough diversionary activities, and activities that provided the same buzz and craic as rioting.

Personal Impact of Interface Violence

Although many of the young people claimed to enjoy getting involved in interface violence to relieve their boredom, it was clear from our interviews that the resultant hostility and tensions between communities also had a wider negative impact on the lives of young people. A large number of the young people felt that their community background was a significant factor in determining the places that they could travel to and the types of resources that they could access. The limitations on the movements of young people because of ongoing sectarian tensions were highlighted in a recent survey of young people in North Belfast (Byrne, Conway and Ostermeyer 2005). This found that 38% of young people said their community background affected where they met friends, while 36% said their community background affected whether they would go to the cinema or which leisure centre they felt they could use.

All of the participants in this research recognised that some local facilities and amenities were effectively inaccessible to some of them because of where they lived or which community they came from. Several issues related to this sense of fear that emerged in talks with young people living in interface areas. Many spoke about the impact and effects that the violence had on them, with a frequently cited concern being a sense of unease felt by those living on or near to an interface. As one 17 year old male in the Fountain stated:

You are worried about getting a kicking like, it does worry you. It is life like (Protestant male).

Similar opinions were expressed in various areas of North Belfast:

We can't even go to the cinema, if we go, we are chased out (Protestant female), while a friend stated simply: *We can't get anywhere* (Protestant male).

Young people from both main communities felt these restrictions on their movement and young people were aware of the dangers of moving outside of their area. One male from the New Lodge stated that such was his fear that he would not use the leisure facilities at the Grove Leisure Centre (the nearest public swimming pool) a few hundred metres away. Other young Catholics in the New Lodge and Newington expressed similar views that they could not use the Grove Leisure Centre, because if they did they *'would get stiffed'*. All of the main leisure facilities or centres were perceived to be claimed by, or belong to, one community or the other. The young people either felt safe using them and therefore had access to a facility or felt completely excluded from accessing a local resource.

For many of the young people, prominent local landmarks might be identified as an informal boundary marker and therefore indicate the limits of safe movement. One young man from Newington noted:
We can't walk past that old factory [on the Limestone Road], while his friend agreed: *They would look at you as if you had two heads* (Catholic male).

In some extreme cases young people felt unable to leave their estate, as they believed they would be singled out for attack. This inevitably restricted the range of activities that they could take part in and, in the case of young people living in the Fountain, even prevent them from accessing the shops and leisure facilities in the city centre. Some young people referred to themselves always being on the lookout and aware of potential danger, thus highlighting the risk many young people feel they are at:

I suppose you could say you are always intimidated, always looking over your shoulder as a guy. As a Protestant you are singled out (Protestant male).

In other cases the young people stated that they could remember where violent incidents or attacks had occurred in the locality and therefore would think twice about entering such locations. One young female noted in a matter of fact manner that it was just:

Something you think about (Catholic female).

Many young people stated that they would only enter certain areas if they were in a crowd and thus perceived that there would be *'safety in numbers'*, but some of the young people said they would only be prepared to access certain facilities if it was part of an organised school activity or if they were accompanied by a youth or community worker. However, distinct gender differences were noted in relation to feelings of safety in movement. Many of the young women said they were more likely to make use of more distant social space and leisure facilities than males, as they felt less of a target than did many of the young men.

Many young people referred to a variety of ways in which they felt they could be identified and therefore become targets. Some of the most obvious means of classifying young people are by their school uniform and types of sports clothing, such as Celtic or Rangers tops, which they wear. Young people in Tiger's Bay, for example, highlighted the importance of school uniforms as a marker of identity and none of the interviewees said they would wear their school uniforms at the nearby Yorkgate Centre. This is a major shopping-centre with a cinema and numerous fast foods outlets, which was in close walking distance to Tigers Bay, but closer still to the Catholic New Lodge area. Young people from Whitewell and White City also referred to the difficulties of travelling to and from school wearing a school uniform, and one of the interviewees in Whitewell had been beaten up while waiting for a bus in his school uniform. Similarly a group of young women in Whitewell said they felt uncomfortable using Irish names in a nearby shopping centre as this clearly identified their community background.

While names, sports tops and school uniforms are all well-established means of telling identity, the young people also referred to a variety of more idiosyncratic ways by which community background would be identified. These included such features as the way hair would be dyed, the type of hairstyle that was worn and the way a baseball cap would be folded. These all appear to be very localised, and probably very transitory, means of community ascription, but nevertheless highlight the importance among young people of both being able to identify someone else's community background and, when necessary, to disguise one's own background for reasons of personal safety.

City Centre Violence

In recent years the media has highlighted an apparent high level of violence and disorder in the city centre of Derry Londonderry. Newspaper reports and comments by young people in the city suggest that violence, assaults and fights were commonplace events. In contrast there has been little publicity about problems of violence in Belfast city centre and the young people we spoke to did not make any extensive or specific references to concerns about their safety in the city. A report by University of Ulster (2003) commissioned by Belfast City Council notes that in general young people considered the area around City Hall as a neutral and accessible venue where young people from all areas could meet and 'hang out'. However, personal safety was a major issue for young people congregating in the city centre of Belfast, particularly at night. This suggests that the greater size of Belfast might provide some measure of safety, but also that safety remains an issue, even if physical attacks are not widespread.

Some evidence of the scale of violence in Derry Londonderry city centre can be found in PSNI statistics for the area. Between 1 May 2001 and 30 April 2002 the PSNI recorded 1,948 assaults in Foyle District Command Unit, 811 of these (42%) were within the city centre. More than half of the assaults in the city centre took place on Waterloo Place and Strand Road, while 56% of city centre assaults took place on the street and 44% occurred in or outside commercial premises. The vast majority (70%) of victims were aged 18-35, while 12% of city centre assaults involved the use of a weapon or dangerous object. The young people in Derry Londonderry who were consulted as part of this research also tended to consider the city centre as a location where trouble was common. Some of the young people we spoke to in the city regarded the city centre as *'threatening'* at night-time. One young male, aged 17, made the point that the city centre was an area where you would not feel safe on your own especially at night:

I wouldn't go there myself at night (Catholic male).

He referred to incidents that his friends had been involved in and also identified areas where they had been attacked. Although not everyone agreed that the city centre was dangerous, those who acknowledged the problems of violence identified the area around Waterloo Place as a particularly difficult area and where most of the fights took place. At the same time the one factor that was identified as creating a wider risk of violence was alcohol. Throughout the discussions it became clear that many of the incidents in the city centre were the result of excessive alcohol consumption, rather than related to any sectarian motivation or intent:

I think it's mostly drink ... I don't think they know what area they are from (Catholic male).

Alcohol was also a recurring theme when talking to some young people who had been arrested and were now on probation for violent behaviour in the city centre. One young male said he had been arrested for fighting in town, but was too drunk to remember exactly what had happened. Another young male, also on probation, said he had been arrested *'up at the city centre'* for biting a policeman after a night out. In some cases the young people spoke of the sheer viciousness of the violence, and at the same time they recognised that they were likely to be involved as victims as well as perpetrators:

Standing on you ... jump on you. Definitely. You go to the ground and all you can do is curl up in a ball ... When I was fighting I had to be dragged off boys ... my mates were dragging me back ... you keep on going until the boy is beating you is beat ... there are no gentleman's rules like ... they knock you down, you get back up (Catholic male).

Numerous other interviewees commented upon the ferocity of attacks. This was also highlighted by the head of the Accident and Emergency Department at Altnagelvin Hospital, who said that Derry:
Was no different to other towns or cities, but the degree of violence being used nowadays was particularly disturbing (BBC News 10 March 2004).

He also referred to people having had their faces smashed with bottles and *'people having had their heads stamped on'*. One seventeen-year-old male talked about the fights that occurred, although he felt that they were not too serious as knives tended not to be used, although he acknowledged that bottles were commonly used as weapons. Some young people believed that there were groups of young people going around specifically with the intention of starting fights and causing trouble. However, others felt that this was a minority of people:

Most people go out to enjoy themselves, but there is a minority that keep giving the centre a bad name (Protestant male).

The majority of participants said that, while they were aware of high levels of reported violence in the city centre, this did not deter them from going out to socialise in the area. Some had obviously given the problem more thought and while they recognised that alcohol was one factor in the violence, also noted that not all young people would be similarly at threat from violence:

At the end of the day, it depends who you are ... each young person is different ... if you get on with your stuff and get on with everybody you go down without being afraid ... if you are a wee hood, and the 'Shinners' are after you for doing drugs or joy-riding ... the city-centre is not the safest place to be ... you are looking over your shoulder (Catholic male).

This suggests that some young people may be vulnerable in the city centre area because of what they are doing or because they have made enemies through their activities, rather than being at the risk of random violence, therefore most people would have little reason to be afraid of attack in the city centre.

Intra Communal Violence

Another aspect of violence and disorder was the extent of such problems within particular estates involving young people from the same community. Young people often referred to rivalry between groups of males from within the same area or from nearby areas from the same community background. In Derry for example they spoke of rivalry between youths from Galliagh and Cairnhill in the Greater Shantallow area, while in North Belfast similar rivalries were discussed between Newington and Ardoyne.
The Galliagh estate on the edge of Derry Londonderry seemed to have more problems with intra-community fighting compared to some of the other areas in the research. The survey conducted by Off the Streets and ICR in Galliagh indicated that 50% of the sample (209 young people) knew someone who had been involved in fighting with people from the

same area, thus highlighting the scale of such events. On one occasion, an interviewee showed up with a black eye and bruises, this prompted a discussion as to what had happened:

I was fighting last night ... stupid stuff ... we battered his friends, and then he saw me on my own ... two of my friends battered one of his friends ... and then they singled me out (Catholic male).

It was accepted that this was how fights tended to start in many cases: one person is the target of violence and in response his friends would search for the perpetrators and attack them in turn. In many of the conversations with young people fights were described as commonplace events, and these mainly involved clashes between gangs or groups of young men. In many cases the violence began for no apparent reason or without any serious flashpoint. One male described the fights as being over:

Stupid things ... it all starts ... alcohol, that it was it is ... sometimes it starts when people start slagging (Catholic male).

A group of young women, aged 15-17, said that young women were also involved in fights and sometimes drinking aggravated this involvement. However, it was young men who were regarded as the main protagonists and participants in fights. While some of the young men said that fights did not take place on a regular basis, one of those interviewed expressed surprise when asked whether these fights were common:

There's more than one every weekend ... there'll be hundreds of fights over the weekend ... definitely (Catholic male).

This perception of the frequency of fights and a sense that violence erupts with very little provocation could possibly explain the large number of young people in Galliagh who said they did not feel safe walking in the area at night. Fifty two percent of young people said they did not feel safe in the area if they were alone at night during the week, while 60% felt unsafe alone at night at weekends. However, only 20% said they felt unsafe in the area if they were with friends.

There was a mixed response in the areas of North Belfast in which we spoke to young people in relation to issues of intra communal violence. In the case of Sunningdale, young people referred to fights taking place within the area, but they claimed that these often involved young men from the wider area. The survey in Sunningdale revealed that half of the young people who responded referred to fighting with 'people from same area' as a problem, this was more than the number of people who cited problems of graffiti, vandalism and fighting the police. In the New Lodge area the young people did not express any fear about walking in their own area at night. One young man said that *'nothing happens that doesn't happen in other places'*. There was no unease about the area as such and *'no hassle'*. Overall they felt safe in their area, and felt that attacks *'didn't really happen here'*. In the Whitewell area young people did acknowledge the problems of fighting among young people, but referred to these as being about *'stupid stuff'*. Such fights were often with groups from other predominantly Catholic areas, but they were not seen as serious issues and it was felt that such fights were often fuelled by alcohol. One interviewee described how such clashes might start from very little more than the mere presence of young males from other areas, particularly if they were perceived to be showing off in some way:

They would come from other areas, pretending to be big men like (Catholic male).

Thus many of the young people accepted that fighting with people from the same community background did occur in their area. But while some regarded this as a problem, which impacted on their sense of safety, others were more dismissive of the violence and considered it just a normal part of life. It was difficult to gauge how seriously the violence was treated, but some of the young people who had been involved in fights spoke of a limited use of weapons such as knives, but in most cases any weapons used tended to be bottles or fists or whatever was handy. There also seemed to be some differences in the perception of the potential seriousness of the violence based on age and some of the older participants acknowledged that some people carried knives or other forms of weapons for their own safety.

Anti-Social Behaviour

Anti-social behaviour by young people has come very much to prominence as a social problem over the past few years and is regarded in many communities and by many statutory agencies as a serious and growing problem. However, others have questioned whether the notion of a growing problem with disorderly youths is anything more than an updating of a recurrent 'moral panic' of the adult generation understanding the attitudes and behaviour of young people (Cohen 2002). The young people involved in this research were readily aware of the problems of lower level forms of disorder in their areas and of the concept of anti-social behaviour, although it was not possible to establish a generally agreed definition of the concept among young people. The interviews highlighted that the understandings of anti-social behaviour varied between different areas and these ranged from young people hanging around street corners, to drinking alcohol, through to more active forms of causing a nuisance and forms of criminal activity.

The survey in Galliagh established that 67% of respondents recognised that there was 'some' anti-social behaviour in the area whilst 27% said there was 'a lot'. The three most frequently cited activities were graffiti (cited by 80% of respondents), followed by joy riding (73%) and causing damage or vandalism to property (67%). A large majority (63%) of the young people who completed the survey believed that 15-17 year olds were the age group most likely to be involved in such activities. Two out of three respondents (67%) said they knew someone who had been involved in writing graffiti and half of the sample also knew someone who had been involved in fights with people from the same area. Slightly lower numbers (44%) knew of someone who had been involved in joy riding and acts of vandalism.

Similar findings were revealed in the survey conducted in Sunningdale. Both young people and adults were asked about the age of people involved in public disorder and crime and most of them identified young people aged between 12 and 17 year old as the major perpetrators. When young people themselves were asked what types of anti-social activities they had been involved in, the majority referred to such things as dropping litter (50%) and making too much noise (45%), rather than anything more serious.

The research in the different areas established that the young people themselves perceived their involvement in anti-social behaviour to be at the 'lower scale' of activities. This meant that they agreed that they were involved mainly in underage-drinking and congregating on the streets, while others cited drug taking as a common activity: *'drugs, drinking and wrecking things'*. They admitted that such activities often resulted in litter, garbage, smashed glass and a general untidiness. In some cases park benches or places where the drinking had taken place would be covered in graffiti or, in the worst-case scenario, be burnt. But this type of activity was not considered as too serious:
It's drinking in the park, it's not joy-riding or stealing cars (Catholic male).

But in some areas young people were involved in a range of more serious activities including joy-riding, driving 'old-bangers' (cars) and quads. For example, in Galliagh the young people referred to using *'run arounds'*, cars which were bought for around £100 and were driven around without insurance and/or tax. In a small number of cases young people also referred to their involvement in crime such as burglary and arson.

However, regardless of their own levels of involvement in different forms of anti-social behaviour few, if any, young people felt that they would discourage those younger than themselves from getting involved in similar activities. This was because to discourage younger people would be seen as hypocritical:

You can't say nothing, as you've done it (Catholic male).

A similar response was expressed whenever the issue was raised of whether parents should take more responsibility to try to prevent their children from getting involved in anti-social behaviour. The young people believed that they were simply doing what their parents had done when they were younger:

They done the same thing (Catholic male).

As with the issue of involvement in rioting, boredom was one of the prime reasons cited for young people getting involved in anti-social behaviour. Many young people also expressed the view that they were determined to *'carry on'* taking part in the various activities and that it was their choice as *'no-one is forcing you'*, even if their behaviour offended older people. Some of the young people in the New Lodge felt that they were able to get away with such activities as the *'police never come round'*. In contrast in some of the smaller areas covered in the research, such as the Fountain and White City, the young people believed that the levels of anti-social behaviour were relatively low, and it was felt that in both areas the paramilitaries controlled the areas and thus kept such activities to a minimum.

Some of the young people felt that the reputation they had got as a result of the adult perception of anti-social behaviour was unfair and they did not deserve to be labelled in such a way. They felt that they tended to get the blame for all manner of things that went on in their communities but that adults were sometimes more to blame:
Adults think we do mad things all the time (Catholic female).

Some adults are worse than young kids (Catholic male).

In conversations with adults in the various areas, reference was frequently made to the issue of young people congregating on the streets and in local parks or open spaces. While this behaviour was regarded as a problem by some adults, the young people had a very different perspective. In Whitewell one gathering place for young people was a local garage, which belonged to the parents of one of the young people. The only alternative was to congregate in one of the parks, one public space where they felt safe as it was not immediately on the interface. In Derry Londonderry some young people reported that they were always asked to move on when they gathered together, even if they were just 'hanging out'. However, while they did not always move willingly, the problems usually arose when adults were rude to them:

If you are just told to move on, move your arse nicely, you do it ... but if someone comes out acting a faggot (like 'move the f-ck or you are dead') you are gonna start rowing at them (Catholic male).

One woman in Galliagh said that usually when young people were asked to move on they were OK about it, but they just kept moving around the estate and eventually they would return to somewhere they had been moved from:

You always know one person (in the group) ... and you pull them aside ... and say to them go on ... or come to a stage where you say to them keep the noise down, stand here if yous want, keep the noise down ... worked here for a wee while ... but then other ones came up then and mixed with them (Catholic adult female).

Although some adults acknowledged that most young people would respond positively if they were spoken to about their behaviour, some adults and community representatives expressed a certain amount of discomfort and even fear about confronting young people. Some adults referred to a reluctance to 'stand up to' young people about their behaviour because of a fear of the possible consequences. One adult referred to his difficulties with the older age groups of young people after he had spoken to them:

I have had my car smashed three times by my own community because I objected to things happening (Protestant adult).
A number of the adults felt a sense of powerlessness when engaging with young people who were perceived to be troublesome, while at the same time insisting that something had to be done. Many adults also expressed a limited faith in the ability of the police to tackle anti-social behaviour, and in particular people spoke of the length of time it took for police to respond to calls. One participant illustrated this:

If you called the police, the police would just think it is a wee misdemeanour, they (the PSNI) won't come out ... they just would say, go tell them to go away, we are to busy, we have something else on, or we try to get out, which means 'forget about it' (Catholic adult).

There was also a sense among many adults that representatives of statutory agencies, whether the police, council officers or others, could not deal successfully with young people involved in anti-social behaviour. They had no real authority over young people and had no respect from them. The poor relationship between the police and young people has been highlighted in recent research (Hamilton, Radford and Jarman 2003), which noted that many young people felt that police officers showed them little respect and in return they had little respect for the police.

The adult perspectives on young people and their behaviour caused frustration among many of the young people, who believed that adults looked on all young people as potential trouble makers or as a threat, and in many cases the young people were made *'scapegoats'* for adult wrongdoings or for the activities of a small minority of young people. The young people interviewed for this research made a distinction between the majority of their age group who just hung about around an area and did not get involved in any real trouble, and those smaller numbers of young people who were known to be involved in 'heavier stuff', which involved activities such as taking hard drugs or joy-riding. These more troublesome young people were often identified as 'hoods', both by adults and by other young people. But some of the young people also self-identified as 'hoods', as is evident in many areas, which are marked out with the graffitied letters UTH or 'Up The Hoods' and which have been interpreted as signs of defiance towards local adult authority (Nagle 2004). However, it is unclear how far the notion of a 'hood' is anything more than a suitable label, whether imposed or adopted. For some the term is used for demonising young people who are perceived to be beyond the control of adult authority. For others it is a useful way of deflecting responsibility for damage and disorder to a more worthy 'other'. For others it may be a badge of honour, whether earned or not.
Anti-social behaviour is acknowledged as a problem in many areas, but defining the term and agreeing how serious a problem it is is another matter entirely. For many young people most complaints about anti-social behaviour exhibit a lack of empathy and understanding of their situation and their activities, and an attempt to exert control over young people who are 'hanging around'. But, although the young people do acknowledge that some activities are less acceptable than others, in turn

the responsibility for such activities is ascribed to a small minority, the 'hoods'.

Alcohol and Violence

Underage drinking featured heavily in the lives of many young people and as a factor in their involvement in acts of violence. This appeared to particularly be the case in Derry Londonderry, as was also highlighted in research by Doherty and McCormack (2003) who carried out a survey of 656 post primary school pupils (aged 13-16) in the city. This revealed that 86% of respondents had drunk alcohol at some time, with 10% having done so on a weekly basis. The reasons that young people gave for drinking alcohol were mainly social rather than any sense of a need 'to escape' from problems. Very few of the respondents said they got involved in fights after drinking alcohol although 32% said that they drank on the street. Similar research carried out in North Belfast on drug misuse among teenagers indicated that many drank alcohol on a regular basis (Radical 2002). The research also referred to the ease by which alcohol could be obtained from licensed premises and how many young children used adults or older friends to purchase it for them.

Our research also found that young people in both Derry Londonderry and North Belfast said they had easy access to alcohol. One male aged 16 said: *If you have the height then you could buy for your mates* (Catholic male), while a young woman similarly agreed that: *You can always get someone to get it for you* (Protestant female). Although many of the young people were cagey about how they got access to alcohol, in some cases it was clear that some adults were willing to deliver alcohol to young people in exchange for money, while others referred to alcohol being delivered to their houses by taxi drivers.

The Sunningdale survey indicated that underage drinking was regarded as a problem in the area, although nearly half the young people (48%) said that it was *'easy'* to get alcohol from pubs, clubs and off-licenses. The discussions with the young people indicated that drinking was seen as a *'buzz'* and *'something to do'* and tended to take place outside, in a park, on a street-corner or in a house when the parents were not present. These findings echo those of previous research (Health Promotion Agency 2000, Radical 2002, NISRA 2002), which also indicated that consumption of alcohol often tends to take place in a 'culture of binge drinking'. The findings from Galliagh are similar to those in the Community Safety Survey (NIACRO 2001). This study found that 75% of respondents referred to 'nuisance behaviour by young people' as the single most serious issue facing the area, with underage-drinking cited by 69% of respondents as one of the main elements of this problem.

The young people involved in this research referred to drinking as simply being something to do while hanging out with their mates and a way of alleviating their boredom. Drinking was primarily an element of their socialising, just as it is within adult culture, the only difference was that they were more visible as they drank when they were hanging out on the streets. The majority of young people therefore did not see why underage drinking should be considered as an annoyance as it was just a way for them to help pass the time. A number of young people stated that they had resorted to drinking in parks and other less public spaces where they could do so in peace. They did acknowledge that it had led to strained relationships between young people and adults in the various areas. This was particularly the case because the young people tended to gather in large groups and congregate in public places, and for many adults groups of young people hanging about together could be seen as threatening or intimidating.

A number of the adults expressed concerns about the effects of drinking on the health of young people and the consequences of excessive drinking on their behaviour and activities. Many adults made the point that underage drinking was now a widespread and common activity and they had real difficulties in finding ways to deal with this problem. In conversation with adults and community workers a certain responsibility was laid at the feet of the parents. One adult asked a simple question:

How do 14-15 year olds get home at night without their parents not knowing they are drinking? (Catholic adult male).

This point highlights one of the recurrent issues raised by various adults consulted in the research, the apparent lack of any responsibility felt by many parents about the activities of their children. There was a feeling that too many young people were allowed too much unchallenged liberty by their parents to do what they wanted and as a result they caused trouble and created tensions within the community. Many felt that the police could offer little in response and it was left to other responsible adults within the community to try to exert some restraint over the activities and behaviour of young people. However, the contrasting view from the young people is that most of the time they are not involved in anything exceptional, most of them do not cause any real trouble and much of what they do is similar to what their parents did when they were young. These two sets of perceptions come from very different perspectives and with little sense of any mutual understanding.

Summary

This review of young people's experiences of and attitudes towards various forms of violence reveals a variety of perspectives. In areas such as the Fountain and Bogside in Derry Londonderry and Whitewell and White City in Belfast interface violence was the dominant type of disorder involving young people. In these areas it was disturbing to note that the fear of attacks and fights had become part of everyday life for many young people. Young people referred to the frequency of interface violence, while attitudes among Protestants and Catholics were noted to be similar, especially regarding the effects of violence and participation. In other interface areas, like Newington and New Lodge, the levels of interface violence had decreased over recent years and somewhat worryingly the young people expressed a yearning for riots and disorder as it provided a buzz and excitement. This seemed to lead to different tension within areas, and a rise of anti-social behaviour within the community.

In places such as Sunningdale and Galliagh, which do not have any interfaces, the levels and experiences of young people of sectarian violence remained low. In Galliagh the forms and levels of anti-social behaviour appear to be higher than in Sunningdale, perhaps in part due to the fact that the area is larger geographically, but Galliagh also seems to experience higher levels of fighting between groups of young people, compared to the other areas under study. Derry city centre has also experienced high levels of fighting and violence, much of it alcohol related due to the proximity of pubs and clubs, establishments which young people seem to have little if any difficulty in accessing. The violence in Derry city centre has attracted attention from the media and for the period studied there were numerous incidents reported. Some young people in Derry Londonderry were reluctant to enter the city centre at night due to fear of attack.

This section highlighted that complaints of boredom and *'lack of things to do'* featured heavily in the discussions with young people as factors that encourage their participation in forms of violent behaviour. This issue will be considered in more detail in Chapter 5, however, before that we focus on issues related to different experiences and understanding of violence by young men and young women and consider in some detail the perspectives of young women.

4. Gender and Violence

Previous research on young people and anti-social behaviour and violence has identified young people as both victims and perpetrators of violence and disorder (Hansson and Conway 2005). However, women's relationship to violence has largely been seen as one of victimhood, and women are often seen as passive victims without any real sense of agency. They are too often regarded as the sisters, wives, mothers and daughters of male perpetrators of violence and are rarely seen as actively participating in anti-social behaviour and violence. Jarman (2005) also notes that:

In much of the recent writing and in most of the policy responses to problems of anti-social behaviour, there is an inappropriate use of the term 'young people' which effectively functions as a gloss for 'young males'.

Recent disorder in Belfast, where teenage girls were observed taking part in the rioting, has however highlighted the active role that can be played by young women in anti-social behaviour and violence (*Times Online* 13 September 2005). This section of the report is an attempt to address this gender-related disparity and to address previously unchallenged narratives of women's relationship with anti-social behaviour and violence by focusing in particular on the attitudes and experiences of young women.

This chapter builds on previous research on the attitudes to and experiences of violence among young people in North Belfast by providing an analysis of that data from a gender perspective. The initial research (Byrne, Conway and Ostermeyer 2005) was based around a survey of 2,484 young people aged between 14-17 years attending school in North Belfast. For the purposes of this study only the data from respondents who live in the parliamentary electoral ward of North Belfast has been used. The sample has then been analysed to highlight any differences or similarities in young women's and young men's attitudes and experience of anti-social behaviour and violence. The survey data was broken down to analyse not only differences between young men and women but also between Catholics and Protestants. Table 6 highlights the breakdown of the sample by religion and gender.

Table 6. Religion and gender of respondents[1]

Religion	Number of respondents	% of respondents	Young men Number	%	Young women Number	%
Catholic	921	69	347	26	574	43
Protestant	371	28	162	12	209	16
Other	50	3	19	1	30	2
Total	1342	100	529	39	813	61

The majority of respondents in the survey were Catholic (69%), and female (61%). The table shows that 43% of respondents were female and Catholic, and 16% of respondents were female and Protestant. Catholic males made up 26% of respondents and Protestant males only 12%.

Experiences of Violence

A key issue arising from the research was young people's experiences of violence inflicted on them due to their religious or community background. This applies to both young men and women: 32% of young men and 37% of young women claimed to have experienced violence as a result of their religious background. This violence revolves around differing aspects of everyday life, but a particular issue was violence surrounding journeys to and from school. When asked whether or not they had ever been afraid to go to school, 67% of young men and 75% of young women said they had been. Fear among young Catholic women appeared to be more prevalent, with 32% expressing such a fear in comparison with 22% of young Protestant women. Table 7 highlights the respondents' reasons for feeling intimidated.

Table 7. Why have you felt intimidated or scared?

Why do you feel intimidated/scared?	% of young men	% of young women
Loyalist/Republican symbols	8	10
Interface area	13	15
Other school uniforms	3	4
Certain sports strips	2	3
Knowledge/experience of previous incident	10	13
Never feel scared	61	51
Other	2	2

1 Technical note: The percentages have been rounded to the nearest whole number, and thus may not add up to 100%. Missing responses have been excluded from the analyses and tables, so base numbers may not always be consistent.

The results show that 61% of young men and 51% of young women said that they have not felt intimidated at all, but of those who have, the key factors are relating to interface areas and the knowledge or experience of a previous incident. Tensions and possible violence at interface areas intimidated 13% of young men and 15% of young women, while more young women (13%) felt intimidated due to a previous incident that occurred than young men (10%). This is of particular relevance later in the study when it becomes apparent that many young people, and in particular young women, feel that their movements in North Belfast are restricted as a result of violence. The respondents were then asked to identify with whom they travelled to school, and the results are shown in Table 8.

Table 8. Who do you travel to school with?

Travel	% of young men	% of young women
On own	19	11
With parents	26	25
With siblings	9	10
Friends	45	55
Other	0	0

Young women are more likely to travel with friends (55%) than young men (45%), with young men more likely to travel on their own (19%) than young women (11%). Young women were also more likely to refer to attacks on school buses than young men. These attacks on young women seem to be perpetrated by young people in school uniform, and there is a fear amongst young women that they are particularly vulnerable to attack when travelling in an identifiable school uniform to and from school. The respondents were also asked which type of violent incidents they had been subjected to while travelling to school (Table 9).

Table 9. Violent incidents on the way to school

Incident	% of young men	% of young women
Not been attacked	53	47
Bus being attacked	12	24
Verbally abused	11	16
Chased	10	4
Objects thrown	9	8
Beaten up	4	1

The most frequently referred to incidents for both sexes were having the school bus attacked and being the recipient of verbal abuse or 'slabbering', as many of the young people termed it. These two incidents appeared to affect young women more than young men, regardless of religious background, with 24% of young women having had their school bus attacked and 16% being the victims of verbal abuse, compared to 12% and 11% of young men respectively. There was however a larger gap between young Catholic men and women (9% compared to 24%), than among Protestants (19% compared to 26%). More young men than women also referred to being chased (10%), having objects thrown at them (9%) or being beaten up (4%) as the major incidents of violence that they had experienced. The respondents were then asked if they could identify those responsible for the violence they experienced, and Table 10 records the results.

Table 10. Perpetrators of violence

Identify people involved?	% of young men	% of young women
People wearing school uniform	16	30
People not wearing school uniform	26	17
Never been attacked	50	45
Not sure	7	8

It is evident that a much larger number of young women (30%) have been verbally abused or attacked by people wearing a school uniform, which therefore suggests the involvement of other young people of school age. However, only 16% of young men identified people wearing a school uniform compared to 26% who did not wear a uniform. It is a possibility that more of those who verbally abuse or attack young men are from an older, 18 plus age bracket, while those who attack young women are more likely to be under the age of 18. There is also a chance that those who do not wear a uniform may still be of school age but not present at that particular occasion, they may be 'playing truant', or they may be under 18 years old but have already left school.

It may be the case that the uniforms worn by young women are more easily identified as coming from the 'other side', or perhaps both young men and women find it easier to attack young women as there may be a perception that the chance of a possible physical altercation is much lower. This was a view expressed in the focus groups, which will be discussed below. These attacks may also explain the fear particularly among young women at travelling to and from school, and will increase their feelings of having their movement restricted. The majority of young women (66%) said they did not feel intimidated, but of those who were, April to June was the most intimidating period (15%). This may be because of the marching season and the resulting tensions, which are particularly prevalent in certain areas of North Belfast with its high number of interface areas.

This question was widened to include a broader range of incidents of violence which the young people may or may not have had experience of in North Belfast. Table 11 shows the breakdown of these types of incidents experienced by young men and women (some respondents identified more than one incident).

Table 11. Experience of violence

Type of incident	% of young men	% of young women
Sectarian fighting	65	75
Fighting the police	57	63
Interface violence	51	53
Fighting at band-parades	45	52
House petrol/paint bombed	41	48
Attacks on school buses	38	53
Forced to leave home	34	38
Pipebombs	33	36
Fighting within community	30	29
Shots fired at homes	27	24
No experience	16	13
Domestic violence	15	13
Attacks on ambulances	13	15
Attacks on firemen	12	12
Sexual violence	7	8

The most widely acknowledged form of violence among both young men and women was sectarian fighting, which 65% of young men and 75% of young women identified as a major issue. Perhaps surprisingly more young women than young men had experienced fighting with the police (63% compared to 57%) and also interface violence (53% compared to 51%). Once again, more young women (53%) than young men (38%) referred to having experienced attacks on their school buses. More young men than women had experienced shots being fired at houses (27% compared with 24%). In contrast 15% of young men cited domestic violence as affecting them, compared with 13% of young women, although due to the sensitive nature of this topic this is most likely an under-reporting of the problem in the area.

A comparison based on community background showed that more Protestant young people had experienced fighting at band parades than their Catholic counterparts. Among Protestants, more young women (64%) than young men (57%) had experienced this particular type of violence. Within the Catholic community, 64% of young women had experienced fighting with the police, compared to 56% of young Catholic men. The corresponding figures for young Protestant men and women were 62% and 60% respectively.

Effects of Violence

When asked about the effects that varying types of violence had on their lives, half of young men and just under half of young women (43%) stated that the violence had no effect on them. Table 12 shows the different effects of the violence on the young people's lives, and respondents were able to identify more than one effect of violence.

Table 12. Effects of Violence

Types of effects	% of young men	% of young women
No effect	50	43
Restricted travel	27	33
Family/friend injured	22	30
Participated	12	5
Injured/hospitalised	11	5
Scared to go out	7	11
Changed route to school	7	9
Unable to attend school	5	14
Forced to leave area	4	3
Changed transport	4	7
Nightmares	4	8
Changed schools	2	0
Medication	2	3

The main effect of the violence was a restriction on travel within the greater North Belfast area. This restriction on movement was particularly the case for young women, with 33% identifying it as an issue compared to 27% of young men. Young women were also more likely to refer to adverse effects, such as having a family/friend injured, being scared to go out and being unable to attend school. There were however more young men than women who referred to having been injured/hospitalised as an effect of violence, perhaps linked to participation in such activities. When taking into consideration community background, 75% of Catholic young women and 74% of Catholic young men said they were scared to go into certain parts of North Belfast. There was more of a gender related disparity among Protestants, with 62% of young men and only 52% of young women stating that they were scared to go to certain parts of North Belfast.

The issues of violence imposing limitations on people's movements was then broken down further, and the young people were asked to identify in what ways restricted travel particularly affected their lives. Again, respondents could identify more than one way in which the restricted travel had affected them. Table 13 shows the findings.

Table 13. How does restricted movement affect you? Do you face difficulties in your social activities?

Activity	% of young men	% of young women
Travel anywhere	34	35
Leisure	28	31
Meet friends	28	29
Cinema	23	17
Play sports	16	6
Shop	11	13
Work	6	5

A larger number of young women than young men referred to difficulties with access to leisure activities (31%), meeting friends (29%) and shopping (13%). Young men felt the restriction on their movement more in regards to accessing cinemas (23%) and sports (16%).

Involvement in Violence

The young people were asked to state whether or not they participated in acts of violence against other young people travelling to and from school, and if so, which types of incident in particular. The majority among both young women and men (77% and 90% respectively) stated that they had not taken part in any form of violence whatsoever. Table 14 shows the breakdown of the varying types of violence taken part in, with some respondents identifying more than one type of incident that they had been involved in.

Table 14. Incidents participated in

Type of incident	% of young men	% of young women
Have not participated	77	90
Abuse on the street	14	7
Throwing objects at people	10	1
Attack school buses	9	1
Chasing people	6	1
Beating people up	5	1

The most common aggressive activity for both young men and women is verbal abuse or 'slabbering', with 14% of young men and 7% of young women saying they had been involved in this. When this is broken down by community background, there is a wider gap between Protestant male and female involvement than their Catholic counterparts, 2% of Protestant young women said they had taken part in verbal abuse compared to 20% of Protestant young men. Among Catholics, 15% of young women and 6% of young men stated that they had been involved in this type of behaviour. This data also suggests that attacks on school buses are again a prevalent issue, with 9% of young men and 1% of young women having taken part in the attacks.

Cross-community Activities

There was also a difference between young men and women regarding their involvement in cross-community activities and having friends from a different community. Young women were more likely to have a friend from a different community (80%) than young men (60%). There was a relatively similar breakdown when gender was cross-tabulated with religion, with 80% of Catholic young women and 70% of Protestant young women having friends of a different religious background, this compares with 62% of Catholic young men who have friends from a different religious background and 50% of Protestant young men. Respondents were subsequently asked about whether or not they had any cross-community contacts, or indeed if they wished to have them. Table 15 documents the responses.

Table 15: How often do you participate in cross-community activities?

Cross-community	% of young men	% of young women
Weekly	14	18
Monthly	8	7
Daily	4	7
Never – don't want to	26	17
Never – don't know how	19	25
Don't know	28	27

More young women than young men take part in daily or weekly cross-community activities and young men were more likely not to want to take part in cross-community activities than young women (26% compared to 17%). More young women (25%) than young men (19%) said that they had never taken part because they don't know how, which would indicate slightly less hostility to the concept of cross-community work than young men had suggested.

Policing

Young people were asked to outline their attitudes and perceptions regarding the police. The results are shown in Table 11. The majority of both young men (63%) and women (60%) saw the police as partisan, however despite this, young women were more positive in their views on the police than were young men, with 30% of young women considering them to be professional compared to only 22% of men. When taking community background into consideration, 43% of Protestant young women saw the police as professional compared to 25% of Catholic young women.

Table 16. How would you describe the PSNI?

Attitude	% of men	% of women
Partisan	63	60
Militaristic	50	53
Professional	22	30
Helpful	19	26
Fair	16	19
Good Service	16	22
Understanding	14	18

Young women were also more likely to find the police helpful (26%), with 22% of young women stating that the police provided good service compared to only 16% of young men. When asked whether or not they thought the police understood the issues and problems facing young people in North Belfast, more young men (17%) than young women (10%), agreed with this statement. This may be explained perhaps by the fear felt by young women at travelling to and from school, and their sense of having restricted movement through certain areas of North Belfast.

As highlighted above, the issue of travelling in North Belfast and also to and from school, featured highly among young women in particular: 36% of young women and 29% of young men said that the police should concentrate on protecting young people going to and from school. The main concerns for both young men and young women were interface violence and paramilitary activity, with 55% of young women and 48% of young men particularly concerned with interface violence. Domestic violence was also a high priority with 31% of young men selecting it, and 40% of young women.

The respondents were then asked to state their experiences of policing, with individuals allowed to select more than one positive and/or negative experience. Young men were more likely to cite negative experiences at the hands of the police, with 50% stating that they had been stopped and searched for no reason. Perhaps surprisingly, more young men (5%) than young women (2%) claimed to have experienced sexual harassment from members of the police service. Young women were more likely to have had a more positive experience with the police, with 18% saying that the police had helped them and 13% claiming that the police had helped solve a problem for them.

The respondents were asked, 'If you were attacked, how would you find out who did it?', 31% of young men and 23% of young women said that they would find out through friends. The most popular option among young women was to go to the police (42%), compared to only 26% of young men who would do likewise. It was also found that 22% of young men would try and find out themselves, with only 12% of young women doing the same. Young people were also asked about measures that could possibly decrease sectarian attacks in North Belfast. More young men than women advocated CCTV (12% compared to 8%) whereas young women advocated more community relations work (14% compared to 9%).

Regarding authority figures within their own community, both young women and young men referred to paramilitary groups (35% and 42% respectively) and the police (36% and 29% respectively), as being the main authority figures in their community. With reference to the responsibility for the violence in north Belfast a majority of both young men and women referred to a variety of issues (Table 17).

Table 17: Responsibility for violence in North Belfast

Who is responsible?	% of young men	% of young women
Everyone	46	60
Young Catholics	11	8
Loyalist paramilitaries	10	5
Young Protestants	8	7
Republican paramilitaries	7	4
The police	6	6
Other	5	3
Political organisations	4	4
Loyal Orders	1	1

Both young women and men referred to a variety of reasons for violence, such as paramilitaries, police and other factors as being responsible for sectarian violence. 46% of young men and 60% of young women blamed everyone for the violence. Young men also referred to young people, both Catholics and Protestants, as being responsible for the violence, 18% compared to 15% among young women. The paramilitary groups, both loyalist and republican, also featured among respondents' answers regarding responsibility for violence in North Belfast, more so among young men (17%) than young women (9%).

The survey findings highlight some of the differences between the attitudes and experiences of young men and young women to different forms of violence and disorder in North Belfast. In some instances young women appear to have more awareness or experiences of certain types of violence, such as fights at band-parades and interface violence, than their male counterparts. The study also found that more young women referred to insecurity, and feared for their safety travelling to and from school. Young women were also more likely to feel that their movement in North Belfast was restricted due to the high levels of violence. Among young women there was also a more positive attitude towards the police when compared with young men.

Young Women and Violence

This section looks more closely at the findings of the qualitative research with young women relating to their sense of safety and their experiences of violence and disorder. The discussion is drawn both from the wider research findings and from four focus groups conducted with young women in the North Belfast area. The participants were all young women aged between 12-16 years old, and came from overwhelmingly single-identity areas in North Belfast, two Catholic/Nationalist areas, Newington and Ligoniel, and two Protestant/Unionist areas, Ballysillan and Sunningdale.

Fighting and Slabbering

In all of the groups when violence and fighting were discussed it was possible to establish the main references being made to fighting outside pubs and clubs, such as the Pigeon Club in Ballysillan or the Elephant Rooms in Belfast City centre. The young women said that fights could often run on for weeks with friends of someone involved in a fight becoming a target for retribution, as they were seen to be 'guilty by association'. Such fights tended to take place outside of the social venues at closing time when people were really drunk and would often develop in response to verbal exchanges or some form of argument. Some of the young women spoke of young women who simply would go out looking for a fight. It was also suggested by some of the participants that if challenged to a fight you could not back away from it, as you would be seen to be cowardly.

Would get you worked up … If you try to walk away from a fight they would come back and get you … you are forced to stand up otherwise they would think you are scared … they would just keep on coming back (Catholic female).

Few of the young women admitted to having been personally involved in fighting, and such fighting scarcely featured in the discussions with Protestant young women. The group of young females interviewed in the Ballysillan area also referred to the fact that they themselves were too young to get into the pubs and clubs in the area, which probably explains their reliance on anecdotes.

Many of the respondents, both Catholic and Protestant, did however identify 'slabbering' as a problem in their area, and this could occur between friends and also between young women and young men. One young woman defined slabbering as a 'verbal fight'. Alcohol often fuelled 'slabbering', which in turn could lead to physical altercations, and in the Protestant community in particular, drinking at bonfires during the marching season was a salient problem.

One specific type of 'slabbering' involved exchanges of abuse among young women from different areas about their fathers' professed links to different paramilitary groups. Indeed there was a general belief that young people would come into their area from elsewhere, start trouble and then leave again, leaving those who actually live in the area to face the consequences and possible retribution.

Very few of the young women in the focus groups had any direct experience of involvement in riotous behaviour. Among young women in Sunningdale, one young woman said:

The police is too heavy handed … but young men would encourage you to do it and then you would get the blame (Protestant female)

The consensus in the group was that young women would be involved in riots but never on the same level as young men. Among Catholic females the general response was similar, a few young women would perhaps be involved, but the majority would just stand and watch as they felt they *'could not be bothered to get involved in riots'*. It was a sense, both among young Protestant and Catholic females, that if there was involvement in rioting, this was just a way of doing what everyone else was doing.

Contrary to the findings of the survey, the focus groups suggested that the young women had experienced few problems in going to or returning from school. However, this could be due to the fact that most of the young women went to school very near to their home and did not therefore have to walk through any contentious areas. On the other hand there were a number of references made to fighting and violence in school. One young female made the point:

We go to an all girls school, it's very bitchy (Protestant female).

There was some discussion about one girl who had been suspended for three days for fighting, but it was also agreed that this was about *'something stupid'*. There was also a feeling among young females that they were often unfairly treated by the teachers and that this sometimes lead to them 'slabbering' with teachers to make their point, but both Catholic and Protestant females agreed that while 'slabbering' was commonplace, fighting was not really tolerated by the teachers.

Restricting Movement

Even though there was a limited involvement in fighting and violence, there was a feeling among the young women that their movement was linked to the area in which they lived. A common theme appeared to be intra-group rivalry, with areas such as the Ballysillan/Sunningdale and Tiger's Bay/Shankill having particular problems. As one participant said:

You're labelled by where you come from (Protestant female).

The ongoing various paramilitary feuds have also affected the movement of young women. The labelling of young women from different areas meant that some were not only afraid to use nearby facilities that were in the *'other's'* area, but also felt limited in their ability to access resources in a rival area of their own side. This was the case where young women in Sunningdale refused to use the Ballysillan Leisure centre even though it was just down the road. This was notably linked to the loyalist feud and the ongoing rivalry not only between the UVF and the LVF, but also between different factions of the UDA in Tiger's Bay and Ballysillan who had subsequently *'fallen out'*.

This rivalry between different sections of the UDA in Ballysillan and Tiger's Bay also highlighted the broad extent to which movement could be restricted, not simply to the territory of the *'other'* community, but also to sub-areas of erstwhile contiguous single identity areas. Some young women noted that:

If you had friends up from the other end of the Ballysillan Road you couldn't really go up cos of the fighting that was going on up there (Protestant female).

Most of the young women said that they did not discuss politics or paramilitary allegiances in school, and several of the young Protestant women from UVF areas said that they had friends in school who were from an LVF area. It would appear that the loyalist feud was more of an issue outside the school gates.

A common theme among the young Protestants was going to watch the bands, particularly at Ardoyne shops. Violence was cited as occurring not only between rival Unionists and Nationalists at the parades, but also between young Protestant women who would *'slabber'* at each other during band-parades and also at the bonfire sites, both often linked to alcohol. This rivalry was also evident among young women from various Catholic areas. Young women from Newington referred to the sense of 'rivalry' between areas such as Ardoyne and Newington, and also the New Lodge and Divis Flats. However, the young Catholic women, contrary to the findings of the quantitative study, appeared to feel less restricted in their movements, although it is possible that the proximity of Newington to the city centre and provision of numerous buses facilitated somewhat easier travel than for the young Protestant women who lived further from the city centre.

The impact on a sense of restrictions on movement was highlighted by the fact that most of the young women said that their area badly lacked social or sporting facilities. Many said they would welcome a gym, a cinema or a new community centre with easy and practical access. A common theme was disillusionment at the lack of activities in the area specifically for young women, as youth clubs were seen to cater for young men only:

There's nothing for girls, it's mostly boys (Protestant female).

One recurring theme in all of the focus groups was underage drinking. Almost all of the young women in the focus groups suggested that under-age drinking was commonplace in their areas. It was felt that under-age drinking was in large part a response to there being 'nothing to do' in the areas, and there was a feeling that if more activities were aimed at young women, there would be much less under-age drinking:

We don't do anything, sit in the house or stand in the street in the cold with your friends and talk (Protestant female).

Alexandra Park is the only place to go (Catholic female).

Young women were identified as drinking just as much as young men in the areas, and many of the participants suggested that it was easy to get hold of alcohol, usually from older people in the area and from off-licenses more so than pubs or clubs. In general, the young women said they would drink on the streets or in a nearby park if available. This was particularly the case of young women from Newington, who used nearby Alexandra Park, while young women from Sunningdale used Cavehill Country Park, or the 'Glen' (referring to the stream coming down from the Cavehill) as it was euphemistically termed. Young Catholic women appeared to be more likely to go to pubs or clubs in the city centre, such as the Elephant Rooms on Great Victoria Street. The young Protestant women appeared more uneasy about frequenting city centre venues that they perceived had become *'more Catholic'*, and some of them preferred travelling to the Shankill Road where they would feel safer.

Policing and Safety

Almost none of the participants, whether Catholic or Protestant, had any faith in the PSNI as an effective police force and there was a widespread belief that the police represented the *'other side'*. Indeed, attacks on the police were generally condoned.

Now I don't think it was nice the way they shot at the police and all, but petrol bombs and blast bombs are all right (Protestant female).

The young women said the police were not welcomed in most of the areas, and if they were attacked the majority of the young women said they would not report it to the police due to the perception that there was little the police could do. The young women were asked who they would go to if they had been the victim of an attack, most of the participants claimed they would inform their parents or friends, while very few said they would go to the local paramilitaries. This was in the main due to a belief that the punishment would not fit the crime and a fear of what the paramilitaries might do. Despite this however, it was also the general feeling that more police would not improve the situation, but would rather make violent situations worse.

The police would probably encourage it (Protestant female).

In most of the focus groups, regardless of religious background, the participants claimed that they had experienced verbal abuse/harassment from police officers, and there was a widespread belief both among young Catholics and Protestants that the police instigated trouble in their areas deliberately.

We don't trust the police ... they (the police) provoke us...they always go for us Catholics in the park (Catholic female).

Despite the general mistrust in the police and the restrictions many felt were imposed upon their freedom of movement, most of the participants said that they felt safe in their area. One exception was during the loyalist feud, particularly in Ballysillan, when it was cited that it was difficult to go out at certain times, or even to get taxis to certain areas. As stated previously, some young Protestant women said they felt safer going to the Shankill than into the city centre as it was perceived that many of the bars had *'become Catholic'*.

A common theme that did emerge was that wherever there was a park that was used by young people, the young women said they would feel safer if there was better lighting at night-time, as they felt intimidated in the dark:

They should get some lights up there (Protestant female).

In all areas, young women preferred to hang out in large groups for safety, particularly at night, but this in turn created other problems. In some of the interface areas such as Newington, for example, where young women liked to hang out in large groups of nine of ten for reasons of safety, this sometimes led to conflict with local residents about making too much noise:

We are not allowed to stand around in a group...but this makes us feel safe (Catholic female).

This could be said to contribute to the further alienation of the young women from their local community, as even standing somewhere they were sometimes seen as 'being up to no good'. Some of the participants suggested that more CCTV cameras would improve the situation, but others responded that these would merely be something that would be wrecked by young people.

Summary

Even though the research encompassed only a few focus groups and thus addressed only a limited range of young women's experiences it did indicate that young women, just like young men, would be actively involved in a variety of violent and anti-social activities, such as underage drinking and 'hanging around'. The participants appeared to have had limited experience in some of the more openly aggressive activities, but it was clear that boredom, alcohol and the nature of their social geography played a prominent role in explaining young women's experiences. Although safety was an issue, in general young women felt safe in their own residential areas, but they felt less safe when they moved further afield to neighbouring areas, regardless of the religious background.

5. Facilities and Engagement

One of the frequent comments that is made in relation to young people becoming involved in forms of violence and anti-social behaviour is that there are too few facilities or resources available to them and consequently the young people take to drinking, hanging around on the street and engaging in anti-social behaviour in response to the boredom. This has been particularly cited as a factor in relation to trouble that breaks out during the long summer holidays in many of the interface areas. In response, many community based groups focus energies in providing activities and distractions for young people during the summer.

However, the summer is only a small part of the year and a widespread lack of facilities for young people has been noted both by young people themselves and by adults. The limited range of resources can be further restricted by the limitations of a sectarian geography which, as noted in previous sections, constrains the movement of many young people. The limited facilities can also be due to perceptions that available resources are unattractive or inappropriate, are not available at the right times, or are considered old fashioned or target the wrong age groups. This section of the report reviews the attitudes of both young people and adults working with them to the various resources available, it considers some of the attempts to involve the young people in the organisation and decision making and finally looks at levels of cross community contacts among young people.

Youth Facilities

There is one less thing to do - rioting (Catholic male).

One issue that featured heavily in conversations with young people in both North Belfast and Derry Londonderry was the lack of appropriate activities and facilities in their area. Young people repeatedly said that there were *'few things to do'* and that the lack of facilities meant that young people drifted towards the use of alcohol and other anti-social activities, such as interface violence. Young people frequently referred to *'being bored'* because there was *'nothing much happening'* in their area. Many said that the lack of facilities meant that they spent much of their time hanging around with their mates but, in turn this meant that they were seen as a nuisance or intimidating by some adults. Some young people also commented that the reduction in the number of riots and outbreaks of disorder meant that they had less to do now than in the past:

There is no more rioting anymore (Protestant females).

Although the young people frequently bemoaned the lack of facilities in their areas, there were in fact a variety of resources targeting young people within each of the research areas, although the range, variety and quality of youth provision differed. Some organised youth provision was supplied by the Education and Library Boards and in all but two of the areas, Whitewell and White City, there were formal youth clubs offering a variety of activities and facilities. Some areas had multi-purpose community and sports halls as well as a social area for young people. Many church and voluntary organisations also offer activities and facilities for young people from the immediate area, with such facilities as pool tables and computers, after schools clubs and drop-in provisions. Most areas also have various sports facilities, while many groups organise visits and trips out of the area and more extensive programmes for young people, including international exchanges. One group of young men from the New Lodge area complained that there was little for them to do, although they also admitted that there was a choice of youth clubs, football and other sports, while a young woman from the Bogside said that it was difficult for her to comment on the facilities in the area as she had '*nothing to compare*' them to and therefore did not know if they were better or worse than anywhere else.

For those young people living near Derry city centre there was a wider range of accessible activities, although some of the young people living in the Fountain were reluctant to venture outside of their home area for the fear of being attacked. For those living further away in Galliagh, issues of cost and transport were important factors in determining which facilities they felt they could use. Many had to rely on buses or taxis to get to the city centre and therefore were more reliant on facilities in the estate. In Belfast, the proximity of numerous interfaces affects young people's access to many facilities, young people in the New Lodge felt they had no access to a leisure centre, even though Grove Leisure Centre was only a few hundred yards away along York Road, albeit in a Protestant area. Similarly, young people in Tiger's Bay felt that they could not access to the local cinema at Yorkgate, while the recently built all-weather multi-sports facility at the Waterworks was perceived to be only available to Catholics.

In a number of areas church based facilities were popular among young people. In the Tiger's Bay/Shore Road area the older age groups frequented a drop-in centre run by a local church, which has a full time youth worker and is open late on Friday and Saturday nights. This was popular among the 16 year olds and over as a place where they could 'hang out' in a 'safe space', although the centre did also offer more structured activities such as drugs-information and leadership training. The attraction of the different centres depended in part on the hours they were open, in part on the resources they could offer and in part on the approach taken by the staff. In areas such as Whitewell and White City, which had no youth clubs or venues for young people, the only option was to attend a nearby youth club in neighbouring Bawnmore. One young male from Whitewell noted that although they were familiar with the people in Bawnmore, *'we don't know them like'* and added that the club was a *'good bit away'*. Similarly although some young people from the neighbouring White City estate travelled to facilities in other nearby Protestant areas, many preferred to use the local community centre, even though this was limited to two nights a week. The rest of the week was spent hanging around the estate or in friends' houses. These examples highlight the limited extent of many young people's social geography and the parochial nature of their friendships. Thus sectarian differences are only one factor limiting their access to resources and they may be equally wary of using resources in a neighbouring community simply because they have had little contact with the young people in that area.

In almost all areas the young people highlighted what they felt was a lack of appropriate facilities for people aged between 14 and 17 years: *there is nothing for our age group* (Catholic male), while in areas where the young people wanted more facilities, they made the point that it was important that they should cater for all ages: *for older age-groups, not just for younger ones* (Protestant female). Frequent complaints related to centres closing too early, or not being open through the summer, or being closed due to lack of funding. Many young people said that they would prefer a more informal drop-in centre to a traditional youth club, as they felt it would offer them more freedom.

The two surveys, in Galliagh and Sunningdale, both highlighted a sense that the available facilities did not match the interests of the young people (Off the Streets et al 2004; Mourlon and Hansson 2004). In Galliagh just under a third of the sample thought that there was the right amount of facilities in the area, but most of these were in the younger 11 to 13 age group. Only 1 in 5 of the older age groups said they used statutory youth provision, but even fewer claimed to use any of the voluntary youth provision. Overall fewer than 50% of young people said they used any form of youth provision, and a large majority of respondents (68%) indicated that there were not enough facilities for young people in the Greater Shantallow Area. The limited number of facilities was also highlighted in the Sunningdale survey where 93% said there should be more facilities for young people in the area, an opinion that was shared by both young people and adults.

Although the focus of complaints has often been in relation to young people hanging around on the streets, this is not a location of choice for young people to socialise, but one of necessity. Similarly, youth clubs appear to be less favoured than other venues where they can meet friends in an informal setting. For young people in Galliagh the most popular leisure venues were the bowling alley (73%), followed by the Northside Shopping Centre (67%) and Templemore Leisure Centre (66%). Less than one third (31%) referred to youth clubs as facilities they currently used, and no more than one in five young people identified any single such facility. In Sunningdale the young people cited the community centre (65%), the youth club (43%) and the Ballysillan Leisure Centre (20%) as the main facilities they used.

Both surveys also offered a list of possible facilities and asked the young people which they would prefer in their area. The young people in Galliagh identified an ice rink (26%) as their first choice, followed by an outdoor pursuit centre and a soccer or GAA pitch as their priorities, in Sunningdale they favoured an outdoor pursuit centre (24%), a sports club (19%) and a youth club (18%). These preferences are perhaps unrealistic for small areas to provide as local resources, but they indicate that the young people have some clear ideas about the facilities that they would favour. Informally however, many of the young people identified much more pragmatic and realistic demands, they said that they just wanted a safe place to hang out with their friends and have a drink without being hassled by local adults.

This last point highlights a factor that recurs through the research, the poor relationship in many areas between young people and adults. Although many of the young people spoke highly about some of the youth and community workers, many felt there was little sympathy of their concerns and issues among the adult population, for whom young people were little more than a problem. The young people, perhaps not surprisingly, felt similarly towards many adults.

Involving Young People

A number of recent studies have highlighted the importance of consultation with young people and the participation of young people in both decision-making and service delivery in a joined-up manner as important elements in improving the lives of young people (Youth Council for Northern Ireland 2000). Hall (1999) found that the vast majority of young people feel that they are rarely listened to or given any respect and believe that their opinions are generally ignored, except when they are misused by organisations with a political agenda or find themselves castigated by the media. Research has also indicated that young people want to be involved in the planning and structuring of activities and policies which are relevant to them (Community Youth Work Team 2002, North Belfast Community Action Unit 2004).

Some attempts have been made to try to get young people involved in activities and thereby give them more influence in policy development. Derry City Council, for example, established a Shadow Youth Council in 2003. This body has 39 members ranging from 16 to 22 years of age and representing various youth, community, education, geographical and political interests of the wider community. Young people involved in the Council welcomed this opportunity to be included and also the fact that they were being listened to. In Belfast, the Greater New Lodge Youth Forum was established in 2002 to provide young people with input into activities for young people. The Forum organised a conference for 70 local young people over the age of 15 to discuss a variety of issues affecting them in the area. Similarly, youth forums had been established in both Galliagh and the Bogside to further involve young people and attempts have also been made to debate problem issues with the wider community. For example, in Spring 2003 adults in the Bogside were invited to discuss what could be done to respond to interface violence, but according to the young people, this simply turned into a situation where the adults criticised the activities of the young people rather than talking about specific interface issues.

Most of the young people involved in this research were not involved in discussions about policy or decision-making. Rather most intergenerational contacts were of a more pragmatic nature and were largely designed to encourage the young people to look upon their areas in a more positive manner and take part in activities which would improve the local environment. This often includes engaging the young people in various arts projects or involving them in the build-up to the major communal festivals.

One recurrent problem is engaging with those young people who are not involved in any forms of youth projects. This often involves forms of detached youth work, which aims to engage with young people on their own terms and outside of the settings of formal youth work structures and institutions. In many cases these are the stereotypical problem young person, who does not participate in organised activities, but rather is seen as contributing to problems in an area. However, while in some cases the young people may choose to avoid organised youth facilities, in others the lack of facilities helped create the problem. One youth worker in North Belfast noted that the closure of local youth-clubs meant that young people sought other places 'to hang out', often in public spaces such as Cavehill Country Park, and this made it difficult to establish and develop relationships with the young people. Off the Streets in Galliagh aims to engage with young people who reject formal youth facilities and have appointed 'street workers' to establish contacts with young people in the area and engage them in activities to give them a greater sense of pride and connection to their area. This has included getting young people to paint a vandalised electric sub-station as part of the Golden Link festival. One local councillor noted the sustained benefits of involving young people in projects such as this that aim to improve the area:

These (electric) transformers have not been vandalised ... because it was given the power to them to do it, and they done it. They didn't damage something that they had done (Councillor, Galliagh).

Engaging young people in arts projects or projects that have an impact on the local environment are often well received by the young people. The Status Zero project in the Brandywell-Bogside engaged a group of young men in a ten-week video project with Bluebell Arts, which involved them conducting interviews with other people living in the area. In North Belfast young people from a number of Nationalist areas have been involved in designing new murals and worked with graffiti-artists in painting the murals. As part of the launch, a coach was booked to take people on a tour of the areas involved and see the projects first hand. The young people praised this initiative, which brought young people together from a number of different areas.

However, one youth worker noted that it was important to think about who was invited to become involved in such projects. He cautioned against the practice of focusing unduly on some of the more militant groups of young people, who he said were very small in number:

The danger is when you are focusing on them, the ones that are creating problems ... you have to get a balance, you have to accept that alright ... they should be brought onboard and engaged and all the rest of it, but not to the detriment of all the rest of them (Youthworker Bogside).

He said there was a concern that other young people would see this as a reward for anti-social behaviour, while they themselves got nothing for just being 'good'.

One area of activity in which young people were often heavily involved was erecting flags and bunting and building bonfires for the various anniversary celebrations and commemorations. In the Protestant areas the young people were involved in decorating the street for the Twelfth of July celebrations. The Fountain is decked out each August in crimson bunting in the run-up to the commemoration of the Siege of Derry. Erecting bunting and painting kerbstones involves both young people and adults and appears to have widespread support among the local community. Bonfire building keeps many young Protestants active in Belfast in July and in Derry Londonderry in August. The young people often stay up through the night in the run-up to the celebrations and even sleep by the bonfire to avoid it being set alight early. Although the *bonie* (bonfire) was regarded as a major celebratory event and an important part of the local cultural heritage, the young people were not always clear about the reasons for the bonfire being built. Two suggestions were offered, both of which display a distinct lack of awareness of their own culture:

Cause we won the war (Protestant male)
and
Because Catholics have St Patrick's Day (Protestant female)

At the bonfire in Sunningdale in 2004, the young people erected a variety of 'huts', which were segregated by age, with the older age groups having more elaborate designs, where they would meet friends and drink alcohol. The various parades and band competitions over the summer also provided an opportunity for the young people to drink freely and these were also occasions when the adults did not try to stop this form of activity.

It was difficult to identify the same level of involvement of young Catholics in similar commemorative events, although in some areas the young people were involved in erecting Irish Tricolours in time for the Easter commemorations, and in the Whitewell area the young people referred to the Easter Rising commemoration as an important local event. As one young woman put it:

It's the only thing we got (Catholic female)

In some of the Catholic/Nationalist areas in both cities the annual Fleadhs, or community festivals, are attended by large groups of young people. The Fleadhs were introduced in the 1980s to provide an alternative to the rioting that often followed the internment commemoration marches. Similarly, the bonfires that marked the anniversaries have also been replaced in many areas and this was not to the liking of all young people, as was evidenced by the graffiti on North Queen Street in August of 2004, which read *'F-ck the Fleadh, we want our bonfire back'*. Many of the young people admitted that they did not care much for the various events during the Fleadh, as they felt that the performances were not aimed at young people and they also felt that they were not consulted or involved in the organisation of the event. However, they did enjoy aspects of the Fleadh but their interest was more in the parties and the opportunity to indulge in drinking with their mates, rather than for the 'culture':

Good party night. I look forward to it, it will be good craic (Catholic male)

The organisers in turn stated that they do their best to curb underage drinking, but they admitted that they were not very successful in doing so.

Many of the young people interviewed as part of this research said they would welcome the opportunity to be more involved in activities in their areas, and the most successful projects seem to have been those which target young people's involvement from the beginning. But, although more projects are recognising the need to be more open to the ideas of young people, in most cases young people remain disengaged from most community activities. The various festivals are occasions where the young people do seem to enjoy getting involved, but the interest appears to be primarily in the space and freedom it gives them to celebrate outside the constraints of adult disapproval. The public festivals may well be considered an opportunity for adults to shed inhibitions and party, but so too are they a chance for the younger generation.

Cross-Community Work

Recent surveys of young people suggest that despite the high levels of polarisation and segregation in Northern Ireland there is substantial interaction between young people from the two main communities and a high number of young people have friends from the other community. The 2004 Young Life and Times Survey (ARK 2004) for example, indicated that 60% of young people had friends from a different religious background, while Byrne, Conway and Ostermeyer (2005) highlighted the fact that 75% of young people attending school in North Belfast said they had friends from a different community background. However, this figure dropped significantly when the question was asked of those respondents who lived in North Belfast, only 31% of young people living in North Belfast claimed to have friends from a different religious background. This low figure is not perhaps surprising given that throughout this research the young people, particularly those living in interface areas, spoke of the difficulties they have had in associating with young people from different communities and the impact that the sectarian geography had on their freedom of movement.

It is perhaps for this reason that a number of the youth clubs and groups working in interface areas are involved in forms of cross-community work. Young people in the Bogside, for example, welcomed the youth council that had been established in the Bogside-Brandywell-Fountain area and which includes representatives from each area in its consultative work. They believed that the cross-community element was an important step in increasing their input in determining priorities and in establishing better relationships between the areas. However, some of the young people, particularly those from the Fountain, were less optimistic about the possibilities of a cross community forum having any real impact or of the neighbouring communities being able to work together:

Well, for people living here ... and with people from around the Bogside and around the Fountain, it just will not happen. (Protestant male)

People were particularly sceptical about the ability to maintain and sustain cross-community work whenever there was ongoing interface violence and tension between the communities. However, youth and community workers on both sides of the interface were keen to pursue and develop cross-community work. The Cathedral Youth Club in the Fountain, Bluebell Arts in Brandywell and Long Tower Youth Club were working together to reduce the tensions and increase understanding of the different traditions and cultures through a 'diversity through sports' project. The Cathedral Youth Club is also involved in a cross-border project, which has included trips to Dublin, Belgium and to Glasgow, and which has enabled the young people to build relationships with young people from Donegal. This project was very popular with young people in the area:

We want to meet up with people from Donegal and Dublin and all ... that was brilliant (Protestant male).

In contrast, conversations with young people in North Belfast revealed that building cross-community contacts with neighbouring interface areas was often difficult. Young people in Tiger's Bay liked the idea of cross-community work but preferably not with young people from the neighbouring areas, with whom they had frequently exchanged hostilities. Similarly, some of the young people from New Lodge had been involved in cross-community projects through school but not with young people from Tiger's Bay. The Cornerhouse, a cross-community centre on Duncairn Gardens, has involved young people from both main communities in a number of projects, including the Duke of Edinburgh scheme, but although this project started as a mixed group, it had to move to a single identity format as tensions flared in the area.

Even without 'formal' cross-community activities some young people tried to maintain friendships and ventured across to *'the other side'* without fear of attack. In the Alexandra Park area young people from both sides claimed to know people from *'the other side'* and said they *'would speak in the park'*. One young person suggested that going on a residential would help them to meet young people from the other community, which they felt would give the opportunity to *'end up liking them'*. There was also some acknowledgement among some young people that where they lived affected their outlook towards the other community and greater levels of contact would only improve things:

It probably would be different, you wouldn't be as bigoted (Protestant male)

A number of the young people had been on trips with young people from the other community and had interacted without any problems. However, as one young man from White City, who had been on a cross-community trip to Norway with Catholics from the Ardoyne commented, during the trip they had become really good friends but had not kept up the contact after coming back to Northern Ireland. These comments echoed those made by other young people:

When you get home you are not going to do anything' (Catholic male) because it was *'Difficult to keep up the friendship'* and that things would inevitably change *'once back in Belfast'* (Protestant male).

Cross-community work with people from neighbouring interface areas appears to be particularly difficult. However, various groups and organisations were still attempting to bring young people from interface areas together. Attitudes among the young people to such activities varied and ranged from enthusiasm to apprehension. For many there was a degree of caution about mixing with young people from the other community due to the history between the areas and some young people felt that because their area was frequently under attack they had very little trust in the neighbouring communities. It was also difficult to establish what the young people thought might improve the relationships between the two main communities. Their suggestions ranged from the more optimistic, who favoured more meetings and activities involving young people from both sides, to the pessimistic, who advocated building higher peace-lines and limiting any interaction.

Summary

Young people in all of the areas where research was carried out complained about the lack of facilities, although in most cases it appeared to be less the case that there were no facilities, but rather they were not stimulating enough, or they were orientated to a different age group, not in a suitable area, or simply did not meet the needs of the young people. Many of the young people could identify a range of facilities that they would have access to in ideal circumstances, and while some of these would cost considerable amounts of money to provide, others could be met if there was a more serious engagement with the young people to identify their needs.

The most successful interventions by youth, community and arts projects appeared to be those that aim to actively involve the young people from an early stage, and invite the young people to help design and develop activities, rather than simply provide them for them. However, at one level many young people would be quite happy with a safe space that they could use to do little more than hang out with friends.

The sectarian geography and divisions impinge considerably on the lives of young people, through restricting movement, limiting access to resources and generally narrowing their social horizons. While many young people have reported having friends from the other community, they also noted the difficulties in engaging in sustained work with people from neighbouring interface areas, particularly where there has been a history of violence and hostilities.

6. Responding to Violence and Disorder

This chapter looks at a range of responses to violence and disorder by different structures of authority within interface communities. This section begins by focusing on the relationship between young people and the police and at a range of measures that have been introduced in response to violence. It continues by looking at the role played by members of paramilitary groups along the interfaces and then focuses on the work of various restorative justice programmes such as Community Restorative Justice in Derry Londonderry and Alternatives in North Belfast. The final section looks at the introduction of Anti-Social Behaviour Orders in Northern Ireland.

Young People and the PSNI

The relationship between young people and the police in Northern Ireland has been the focus of a surprisingly limited amount of research (McVeigh 1994; Ellison 2001; Hamilton, Radford and Jarman 2003), but this has consistently indicated that young people feel they are treated with little respect by the police and are frequently subjected to forms of harassment. The types of behaviour which young people include within the definition of harassment range from forms of physical violence, through varieties of verbal abuse, to the mere presence of police officers (Hamilton, Radford and Jarman 2003, 2004). Ellison (2001) found that age and appearance, plus locality and social class, were the key factors that young people believed affected how they were treated, rather than simply community or religious background. Similarly, Hamilton, Radford and Jarman (2003) noted that young people generally have a negative experience of the police, regardless of their community or religious background and many felt that the police always assumed that they were up to no good.

The research in Derry Londonderry and North Belfast indicated that most interaction between young people and the police took place when young people were engaged in forms of anti-social behaviour, such as underage drinking and also during situations of public disorder, for example during riots at interfaces. This suggests that the most frequent form of contact involves the police attempting to stop the young people doing something rather than any more positive forms of engagement.

The general attitudes of young people towards the police varied. Some were openly hostile, for example some of the young people in the Fountain referred to the police as a *'joke'* and they claimed that the PSNI had lost all *'credibility'* in their area since the introduction of new reforms. Similarly, young Catholics from Newington in Belfast, said that the police were *'always going to be wankers like'* and *'you just ignore them'*, while young Catholics in Derry said that the increased representation of Catholics in the PSNI had made no difference to the way the police were perceived. They also felt that the PSNI often aggravated the situation in the city centre and contributed to the problem of violence and disorder in the area by their interventions. However, others were more sympathetic. Some young people said that they felt safer knowing that there was a police presence around the city and others acknowledged that the police were sometimes reluctant to respond to calls because they were likely to get stoned or attacked if they did.

In general, the comments indicated that young people in both communities have little respect for the police. In the case of Galliagh for example, when young people were asked who they felt would be most supportive if they were in trouble, only 7% answered the police, while the largest majority answered parents and friends. This feeling of little, if any, respect for the police can also be explained in part because young Protestants and Catholics both believed that the PSNI selected them for harsher treatment than young people from the other community and that the other community was generally treated more favourably.

They [the police] always come down to our side of the park ... never go to their side ... that's a fact (Catholic male).

Young people in the Bogside said the police tended to support those living in the Fountain, as the Protestant population on the city side was dwindling. However, in the Fountain residents felt that they were the ones who were worse off:

If the police were to arrest the young people who are fighting ... the police come up here to pick on families ... the police don't want us here, cause if we weren't here it would make their life easier for their job (Protestant female).

There was also a general perception that the police were often deliberately provocative in their behaviour to try and provoke a response from young people. In some situations the presence of the police in an area seemed designed to do little more than to raise tensions:

There was nothing going on in the Bogside and I saw five land rovers driving in and about the Bog and that is provoking fights ... it is encouraging them (Catholic female).

In other situations the young people referred to the police as:

Harassing ... they would pick fights ... for no apparent reason (Catholic male).

A group of young people in Sunningdale referred to similar contacts with the police, mainly in the Cavehill Country Park, which involved the police:

Hassling us and taking their batons out (Protestant male).

Much of the interaction between young people and the police was described by the young people as *'slabbering'*, which involved an exchange of comments and verbal abuse between police officers and young people. However, slabbering may easily escalate to other forms of harassment, including the young people being chased by the police. In some of the areas young people referred to the chases as being *'good craic'* and this suggests an element of provocation by the young people, again as a means of relieving boredom. Being chased seemed to be regarded as a common feature of interaction with the police when they were patrolling an area, but as some of the young people said:

If they catch you, they would beat the shit out of you (Catholic male).

Others claimed that if the police caught you they were likely to punish you by dumping you in a hostile area:

They would drop you in the middle of the Shankill (Catholic male)

However, none of the group who cited this claim had ever been lifted and taken to another area and this suggests that this claim may be no more than a current urban myth.

Many of those interviewed said they had experience of the police confiscating their drinks and claimed that the police often waited outside a park and other areas where they *'hung out'* simply to be able to take their alcohol. The young people however had experienced a variety of responses after they had been *'lifted'* by the police when they had been drinking. In most cases the young person was merely driven home, but some claimed that they had had to stay in the police station for a few hours, and then, depending what they had done whilst drunk, either meet a probation officer or receive a caution before they were allowed to leave.

Some of the young people spoke of their involvement in more violent clashes with the police that went well beyond the normative *'slabbering'* and chasing. One group of young males who were interviewed in Galliagh were on probation after being involved in an attack on the police at the polling station in Shantallow Youth Club during the Assembly elections in November 2003. One of the group admitted that the youth club *'got wrecked'* when stones and bottles were thrown at the police, but the attack was variously described as *'fun'*, *'a buzz'* and *'good craic'*. A group of young people in the Bogside also talked about being involved in attacks on the police and how these were motivated in some cases by politics and in others by frustration. Some of the young people referred to the police as *'scum'* and said that when they entered the area:

They would get bricked (Catholic male)
and
We would attack them with stones ... sometimes try to steal their equipment (Catholic male).

Some of the young people who had experience of interface violence told of how the police would arrive to break up a riot only for the young people to turn on the police and attack them or their vehicles. When they were asked if they thought it was acceptable to attack a police land rover, the reply was:

Yes, the police would attack us if there's a riot going on (Protestant male).

For some of the young people attacking the police was thus considered acceptable behaviour in some situations, while in some cases the young people believed that the police themselves were responsible for violence commencing, for example if they tried to disperse people from interface areas. Although some of the young men struck up a bravado pose in relation to attacking the police, others noted that changes had occurred in recent years. One young man from the Bogside said he felt that rioting wasn't the same as in the past as there was now a certain amount of fear towards the police:

It's crap these days ... no-one goes up [to the interface-Diamond] anymore ... all young boys are scared ... scared of the cops (Catholic male).

This was particularly the case in relation to protests at various Apprentice Boys parades in and around the Diamond at which there had been a significant police presence in recent years, and which had led to a number of young people being arrested. Such changes might also be related to changes in the underlying reasons for engaging in attacks on the police, with less evidence of any political rationale for violence and more comments that cited violence as a form of *'craic'* or because of hostility towards the police. A representative from the Probation Board said that in most of the cases where clients had received a probation order for riotous behaviour, it was difficult to discern any sense of political motivation. They believed that peer-pressure was a key factor and highlighted that rioting was more likely to start out of a *'hatred'* for the police than out of any political motivation:

I have never heard one of them say I was rioting because I support Sinn Fein and I support the Republican cause ... I have never ever heard that, what I nearly always hear is 'I hate the police they are black bastards' (Representative, Probation Board).

Many of those young people who were critical of the police could see no way in which the relationship could be improved or the cycle of violence be broken. There was also some scepticism at the potential benefits of a greater police presence to reduce the potential for disorder. One young man summed up a general attitude in responding to a suggestion that having more officers on the beat might reduce violence by or among young people. He said simply:

No ... they would be attacked (Protestant male).

The survey of young people in North Belfast (Byrne, Conway and Ostermeyer 2005) highlighted that half of their sample had experienced fighting with the police. While the complex nature of that area and the extensive recent history of interface violence might be considered factors in this number, a similar percentage of young people in Galliagh, which is not an interface area, said fighting the police was a local problem. It was thus evident that the police were not really welcomed by the young people in any of their areas, and if they moved in to stop confrontations on an interface, they themselves were likely to become the focus of attacks.

While the young people were critical of the police in 'harassing' them, many of the adults were critical of the police for not doing enough to deal with young people causing problems. As was noted earlier, in some of the areas the adults were critical of the police for being slow to respond to call-outs to trouble at an interface. In the Fountain, for example, there was belief that the police did not intervene quickly enough when fighting or attacks by petrol bombs affected the area. Some of the young people also felt that in some situations the police did not intervene quickly enough and as a result they were forced to defend their territory. In other areas there was a feeling that the police did not have a high enough visibility or presence, or even avoided an area because of its reputation:

The cops won't come in here, police won't come in ... in 90% of situations (Catholic male).

Other adults felt that the police had a limited impact on anti-social behaviour in their area. They said that while a police patrol might well disperse the young people who were causing problems, they would be back sometimes later the same night, and inevitably the next day, while the police patrols would only occur on an occasional basis. In some areas this meant that people might look elsewhere to deal with local problems but in Sunningdale, although a large majority of adults (70%) said the police did not do enough to control crime in the areas, a similar majority (70%) said they would still turn first to the police to report a crime, while 79% said they would turn to the police to deal with anti-social behaviour.

The relationship between the young people and the police thus came across as strained in all of the areas that were researched. Regardless of the community background there was a sense of victimisation among young people in the relationship with the police. It was also difficult to gauge any idea about how the young people felt this relationship might improve. Most forms of contact had been at street level and this only seemed to perpetuate a cycle of harassment and abuse. While other research (Hamilton, Radford and Jarman 2003; Byrne, Conway and Ostermeyer 2005) has suggested that the police need to engage with young people in other contexts and through more open agendas, the findings from this research suggests that work between local police through such means as visits to local schools and youth clubs, which have tended to take place mainly in Protestant areas, has had little overall impact.

The Police and Young People

In conversation with police officers there was widespread agreement that young people were frequently involved in interface violence, but also a recognition that in many instances such violence was a consequence of boredom and had become an accepted way of life in these areas. Some officers acknowledged that intervention by the police could make a situation worse and they made the point that it was sometimes easier to make inroads in situations of tension if an officer from the Community Safety unit was involved, rather than relying on other officers who might not know the local context or any of the local people:

Other times there has been police from the station ... and they go sort of racing up and things don't go as well, there's ... you know ... because he knows me can relate to us, he will speak to us ... so probably yes... they know your face certainly does help. (Officer Foyle DCU)

Officers in Derry Londonderry made the point that while in some situations ready access to some of the Nationalist/republican areas was possible, they also acknowledged that at certain times of the day or year, particularly when large numbers of young people were about, it was much more difficult:

In general, we are not really welcomed with open arms shall we say ... when kids are at school we can generally go into those estates and go about our business...at summer or after school if you take the vehicles in they get destroyed, if you go in you have to go in with land rovers, because otherwise the windscreens and various things get broken. (Officer Foyle DCU).

This view was also shared by the PSNI in North Belfast, who felt that community involvement officers had a greater rapport with young people than members of response units or tactical support units, as their faces were known by some of the young people. There was however also a general agreement among officers in North Belfast that interface violence had been reduced over the previous years and they felt that this was in part due to the hard work that was being done on both sides of the community, but they also cited the impact of the numerous CCTV cameras across the area (see below).

However, if there was some apparent reduction in levels and frequency of interface violence, it was also clear that this had in part only shifted the problem for the police as they had also noted an increase in young people's involvement in other forms of violence and disorder, particularly in the broad category of offences included under the term Youths Causing Annoyance or anti-social behaviour. Perceived problems of anti-social behaviour have become increasingly prominent in recent years. However it is far from clear how much this is due to any actual increase in criminal or disorderly behaviour among the young, and how much it might largely be due to a greater focus of attention on this 'new' problem.

In an attempt to put the issue of anti-social behaviour into a context, statistics for seven categories of activity were grouped together under the umbrella term of anti-social behaviour. These include: assault, criminal damage, drug offences, burglary, public disorder, vehicle theft, and other offences (threatening behaviour, interfering with motor vehicles, drunkenness). Statistics from the Criminal Justice Policy Division for 1993 to 2002 (Table 18) shows the number of young people convicted of these seven activities.

Table 18. Young People convicted for anti-social behaviour offences 1993-2002

	1993	1994	1995	1996	1997	1998	1999	2000	2001	2002
12-14	116	147	103	111	129	145	119	136	128	102
15-17	716	726	808	811	808	761	639	656	669	627
18-24	3,691	3,386	3,427	3,436	3,225	3,066	2,949	2,767	2,233	2,025
Total	4,523	4,259	4,338	4,358	4,162	3,972	3,707	3,559	3,030	2,754

Source: Criminal Justice Policy Division

The figures reveal that the total number of convictions was fairly steady between 1993 and 1996, but in subsequent years have declined significantly. By 2002 the number of convictions had declined by 29% since 1993, with the most significant decline being among the 18-24 age group. A breakdown for the different age groups in Derry Londonderry for the various types of anti-social behaviour shows the numbers of convictions for each age group over the period 1993 to 2002 (Table 19).

Table 19. Young People Convicted for anti-social behaviour in Londonderry Courts 1993-2002

	12-14	15-17	18-25
Assault	20	119	598
Criminal damage	34	102	310
Drug offences	1	17	273
Burglary	32	160	268
Public disorder	18	187	886
Taking vehicle w'out owner consent	2	45	179
Other	4	12	25
Total	111	642	2,539

Source: Criminal Justice Policy Division

In Derry Londonderry the convictions for 12-14 year olds show that activities such as burglary and criminal damage account for the highest percentage of convictions, whereas among the 15-17 age-group half of the convictions are for public disorder and burglary. More than half of all convictions among 18-25 year olds are for assaults and public disorder, while proportionally convictions for burglary are fewer.

A similar picture is evident in Belfast where criminal damage was high among 12-14 year olds, as in Derry Londonderry, however assaults are the most common conviction among 12-14 year olds (Table 20). In the 15-17 year olds, assault, criminal damage and public disorder were the most common offences. As in Derry Londonderry, among 18-25 year olds public disorder was the most common offence followed by assault.

Table 20. Young People Convicted for anti-social behaviour in Belfast and Newtownabbey Courts 1993-2002

	12-14	15-17	18-25
Assault	101	481	2219
Criminal damage	119	477	1430
Drug offences	5	90	980
Burglary	92	356	1007
Public disorder	49	471	2820
Taking vehicle w'out owner consent	26	388	1128
Other	6	40	117
Total	408	2,303	9,701

Source: Criminal Justice Policy Division

Whilst the overall numbers of young people convicted of criminal forms of anti-social behaviour have declined over recent years, there appears to be a growing problem of young people causing annoyance through a variety of relatively low-level activities, which while not necessarily being criminal offences, do cause feelings of intimidation and harassment among older members of the community. The issue of Youths Causing Annoyance (YCA) has become one of the most contentious policing issues in an area like North Belfast. The police reported that they received 1,900 calls about such incidents between 1 April 2003 and 31 October 2003, compared to 1,070 for the same period in the previous year, an increase of 57%. The PSNI recorded over 7,000 reports of young people causing annoyance in North Belfast over a three-year period (2001-2004). A broad classification of the types of activities that were being reported indicates complaints about a varied pattern of young people's behaviour (Table 21). The three most commonly cited activities were young people under the influence of alcohol or other drugs, young people causing a general disturbance by playing loud music or being involved in rowdy behaviour, and young people causing a specific disturbance such as harassing or intimidating staff in a shop. However, it is also worth noting that the fourth largest category is a catch-all category for behaviour that causes a general annoyance, but without much detail of what such behaviour is. This suggests that a large number of adults seem to find almost any activities by young people in public space to be a problem.

Table 21: Complaints of Youths Causing Annoyance in North Belfast, 2001-2004

Category	Number of Complaints	% of Total
Under Influence Alcohol or Glue	1037	14.3
Causing a general disturbance	881	12.1
Causing specific disturbance	767	10.6
Not enough information to classify	578	8.0
Trespassing	470	6.5
Throwing objects at traffic	467	6.4
Throwing objects at buildings	433	6.0
Interface disturbances	431	5.9
Malicious damage	421	5.8
Riding Quads/skateboards etc	279	3.8
Youths gathering in public	243	3.3
Playing football/cricket in street	229	3.1
General intimidatory behaviour	197	2.7
Fireworks	138	1.9
Setting fires	107	1.5
Fighting	100	1.4
Remainder	494	6.8
Total	7,272	100

Although many young people would claim that too often they are accused of anti-social behaviour when they are doing little more than hanging out with friends, the scale of complaints, and the frequency with which complaints of anti-social behaviour are made to the police, suggest that many adults find a wide variety of young people's behaviour problematic. It is therefore worth noting that the 2003 Young Persons Behaviour and Attitudes Survey indicated that 21% of 11-16 year olds admitted to having 'attacked, threatened or been rude to someone', while 19% admitted being 'noisy or rude near home causing complaints' and 18% admitted to being 'noisy or rude in a public place' (NISRA 2003), thus suggesting that many young people acknowledge engaging in forms of offensive behaviour.

In the interviews with the PSNI in North Belfast and Derry Londonderry it emerged that alcohol consumption was a key factor that increased the range of potential problems with young people, and these included not only young people as perpetrators of alcohol related violence, but also as victims of alcohol related violence:

They [young people] just cannot handle it ... the state of some of them when they come out, they can't remember. When they come in here and have been badly assaulted they can't remember who did it or how it happened or whatever ... I think alcohol's got an awful lot to do with it, easy access and young people getting into licensed premises ... they shouldn't be there (Officer Foyle DCU).

The police in North Belfast made reference to their interactions with youths, which they classified as Youth Causing Annoyance:

There are a number of places that young people would congregate and we would then have to deal with that problem - then we would see a different side. They [the young people] would argue that they are just standing not causing any annoyance but the neighbours would say they are very loud whenever the police aren't there (Officer North Belfast DCU).

While the police are often called out to respond to problems of disorderly and/or drunken youths, they have also attempted to respond to the problem by other means than by direct intervention. In June 2004 the PSNI in North Belfast launched an initiative called 'Operation Alco-pop' which targeted local off-licenses in North Belfast over a period of two weekends. The operation involved four teenagers going into off-licences to try to buy alcohol. Eight off-licenses in North Belfast sold alcohol to the teenagers and these premises were then approached by the PSNI. The police also made 70 seizures of alcohol from young people and 23 young people were reported to the Youth Diversion Officer (*BBC News* 8 June 2004, 'Crackdown on underage drinking'). Such initiatives attempt to reduce the problem of under-age drinking and associated problems. This approach also indicates that responding to problems of youths causing annoyance and alcohol related disorder is much more than a criminal problem and is not something that can necessarily be addressed through the criminal justice system.

Nevertheless, in some cases the excessive use of alcohol by young people can and does lead to serious forms of violence which requires the intervention of the police. This has been most apparent in locations such as Derry city centre, where a high level of violent assaults has been noted in a number of recent years. One police officer made reference to the high number of assaults which had occurred in the Derry Londonderry city centre in 2002:

Last year alone we had a total of 2,000 assaults within the Foyle DCU ... I think that something like 46% of those 2,000 assaults occurred within the city-centre outside business premises and licensed premises ... that was five a day (Officer Foyle DCU).

Another officer in Derry Londonderry felt that a specific number of factors contributed towards the violence in the city:

We would see the level of city centre violence as being a combination of factors. Probably, obviously economic and social factors and with the troubled history of the city ... the city centre is very busy with regards to night life and you have then at night a lot of young people from 16 to 30's, coming out of pubs and clubs (Officer Foyle DCU).

The police felt that most of the attacks involved young people, either as victims or perpetrators. The attacks were viewed mainly as random and rarely had a sectarian motive. One spate of attacks was referred to where the motives appeared to be completely senseless:

There was a gang of youths operating, called the 7-up club, and what they were doing was, they were picking, for example, every 7th male wearing a tie ... and that was the person who was subsequently attacked (Officer Foyle DCU).

As a way of combating such attacks the police adopted a more visible approach where they made a point of being present and being seen:

There were complaints that the police were not doing enough ... we then said let's put in a soft approach to it ... lets say seven or eight police officers in high visibility jackets, so when we walk out from the station on a Saturday night everybody knows we are out ... our main priority is to reduce assaults and obnoxious behaviour (Officer Foyle DCU).

As was the case with anti-social behaviour, the police in Derry Londonderry highlighted the need for a more coherent and joined-up approach to the violence in the city centre, which involved more than just the PSNI. They also noted that there had already been some positive initiatives such as improved training of door-staff at the various pubs and clubs and the introduction of plastic mugs rather than glasses before closing time. A representative from the City Centre Initiative (CCI), a body set up by Derry City Council and the Chamber of Commerce, referred to the city centre as having a 'fear factor' for many people, who may not have been affected by violence themselves but have read or heard about it. While the representative criticised some media reports describing the city as a dangerous place, he also acknowledged that there were problems and these could only be addressed through broader partnerships and 'joined up' approaches. One recent example that was cited was an initiative between CCI and Translink to start a night bus scheme for areas outside of the city centre, which was set up to prevent people from 'hanging around' after closing time and waiting for a taxi.

CCTV and Violence

One prominent response to the persistent problem of violence in many interface areas in Belfast and of disorderly behaviour in Derry city centre and other town centres has been to install a network of close circuit television cameras. CCTV has become an increasingly frequent response to crime and disorder both in Northern Ireland and across the UK more generally, although the effectiveness of such technology is far from certain (Gill and Spriggs 2005; Welsh and Farrington 2002).

In Derry Londonderry the City Council installed twenty-six CCTV cameras in 2000. The CCTV was used by the PSNI to conduct forty-two 'street arrests' in 2002 and 2003 (55% of all cases of street arrests) of people involved in disorderly behaviour and assault (*Londonderry Sentinel* 16 July 2003). The police in Derry Londonderry considered the CCTV to be helpful in the policing of the city centre and in relation to the violence in the town. CCTV was also seen as being of great assistance, providing them with a greater overview of the area, but felt that it had to be used in conjunction with 'ordinary policing'.

However, the Pat Finucane Centre, a local human rights organisation, has been critical of the scheme, particularly the lack of any independent monitoring of the CCTV, and they have also asked for clarity surrounding the hours of use of the CCTV. In particular they mentioned cases where CCTV footage had been cited in a local paper and where the individual in the picture was wrongly accused of shoplifting. In contrast, staff at the Rainbow Project, a gay men's health project, noted that assaults on gay people had decreased since the mid 1990s and many young gay men who had been victims of attacks were in favour of the CCTV scheme which they believed had a positive impact on the reduction of attacks:

It has reduced city-centre assaults, it has also created a sense of security among quite a few people that I know that frequent the bars, frequent the centre, they are a bit more confident about coming out on the town. Without it 'ghettoisation' would have been complete, we would have arrived and departed by taxi and would not have been anywhere else in town except the gay bar (Rainbow, staff member).

The use of CCTV has also become widespread in interface areas across North and East Belfast. In 2002 twenty-five cameras were installed at the main interfaces in North Belfast, and a number of others have subsequently been installed in other locations. A representative from the PSNI in North Belfast felt that a reduction in violence in the area had been partly due to the cameras, particularly on Limestone Road. The police have also used CCTV images to identify and prosecute individuals involved in public disorder, a practice that has been used elsewhere (Carling et al 2004). A number of police officers have highlighted the difficulties they have in managing disorder at interfaces and in particular the difficulties in arresting people in times of tension. They have increasingly come to rely on CCTV and video to record activities and only attempt to make arrests in the aftermath of the violence.

A community worker on one of the interfaces in North Belfast spoke of the effectiveness of the CCTV cameras and had also used such images, in conjunction with the PSNI, to show young people in the area how detailed the pictures were, thus hoping to discourage young people's participation in disorder. However, other community workers were sceptical of the value of CCTV and believed that their presence did not deter young people from becoming involved in interface violence. Similarly, a number of police officers in North Belfast made the point that there had been a reduction in interface violence before the introduction of the CCTV and that it was difficult to determine whether or not CCTV was responsible for this.

Our research found that young people in Derry Londonderry were sceptical about the effectiveness of the CCTV (see also Zurawski 2005). One 18 year-old male who had been assaulted in the city centre said that the CCTV cameras had not been of use to him when he was attacked as the police said that they did not film his assault. This he felt was not an unusual occurrence:

If you ask anybody who has been assaulted in town, it is always 'sorry the camera was turned the other way' (Catholic male).

Other young people highlighted that the positioning of the cameras was too noticeable and they didn't act as a deterrent to stop attacks it just meant attacks occurred out of their viewing:

Where the cameras are, are obvious, because you can see them ... if people know where they are, they know where to look ... if they are going out to hit somebody, that is what you are going to do, you are not going to do it where the cameras can see you (Catholic male).

Young people were also critical of the cameras as they felt that they had only been erected *'to make shop-keepers happy'*. However, others were more positive about the CCTV. One young male, aged 17, made the point that the city centre in Derry Londonderry was not as bad as it used to be because of the stronger police presence and the introduction of CCTV:

You have to watch yourself ... CCTV works (Catholic male).

It was difficult to obtain views from any of the young people living in interface areas in Derry Londonderry. The young people in the Fountain did not appear to be particularly aware of the CCTV in the city centre, while young people in the Bogside believed that the installation of surveillance equipment on Bishop Street was just another means of monitoring and spying on their community. In contrast, young people from both communities in Belfast felt that the cameras had made a difference. A group of young males from the New Lodge said that the cameras prevented most of the violence in neighbouring interface areas, and in White City the cameras were seen as being the reason for the reduction in incidents and riots on the interface. One 13-year-old female from White City said:

See where we showed you the cameras, see before they were there ... it was every day, every night (Protestant female).

However, some of the young people were not as sure of their success, and voiced similar criticisms as the young people in Derry, as to their position and ability to capture events,

If something happens, the police says the cameras don't pick it up or anything ... and the cameras are supposed to be on 24 hours a day (Protestant male).

It seemed that the presence of CCTV in both Derry city centre and on the interfaces of North Belfast generated mixed responses. For some young people the introduction of CCTV has created a deterrence towards engaging in forms of violence as there was a feeling that you could get caught on camera and therefore face a prosecution. However, other young people were sceptical of how effective the cameras really were, especially when they were aware of key events that had not been recorded. Something of this ambivalent and uncertain attitude to the benefits of CCTV was captured in the contrasting responses to CCTV in the survey of young people in North Belfast (Byrne, Conway and Ostermeyer 2005). Although only 10% of respondents believed that 'more CCTV' would help to reduce sectarian attacks in the area (17% of Protestants compared with 6% of Catholics), some 44% cited 'more CCTV' as the single factor that would improve policing in the area (favoured by 56% of Protestants compared to 40% of Catholics).

Despite the prominent role given to CCTV as a means of both deterring acts of violence and providing evidence for prosecution, there is some considerable uncertainty among young people, community workers and police officers as to how effective the cameras actually are. However, such uncertainty may nevertheless be a factor that works in favour of the technology, as it retains the potential to record acts of violence.

Young People and Paramilitaries

When considering that CCTV has the ability to deter through its mere presence, it is also important to consider other factors that may create a sense of concern for those involved in acts of violence. Thus it is important to consider the role of paramilitary organisations in relation to young people's experiences of violence and disorder. Although the main paramilitary groups would regard responding to the violence of the state or the other community as their main objective, they also play a role in imposing forms of order on members of their own communities. This frequently brings them into contact with young people. In some cases the paramilitaries target young people because of their involvement in perceived acts of crime or anti-social behaviour, in others they may aim to recruit young people to the organisations and they may also use young people informally at times of inter-communal tension and disorder.

Paramilitary groups exercise influence in all of the areas that were researched and have frequently resorted to the use of violence against young people while claiming to be responding to popular pressure from within their own communities. Both loyalist and republican groups have participated in 'punishment' shootings and beatings (Knox and Monaghan 2003). Tables 22 and 23 (below) show figures for the number of punishment shootings and assaults on people under 25 years between 2002/2003 and 2004/2005. The under-25 age-group makes up the largest share of all victims of shootings for the period studied, although there has been a decline over the three year period in the total number of young people being shot and the proportion of young under 25s to all ages. In 2002/2003 young people were the victims of 62% of such shootings, this declined to 58% the following year and 53% in 2004/2005.

Table 22. Casualties of Paramilitary Style shootings

	2002/2003		2003/2004		2004/2005	
	0-25	All ages	0-25	All ages	0-25	All ages
Northern Ireland	102	165	87	149	49	93
North Belfast	30	42	7	22	12	24
Derry-Londonderry	2	3	3	3	-	2

Source: PSNI, Central Statistics Unit

Changes in the number of assaults are less clear, although there was a substantial decline between 2003/2004 and 2004/2005. The under-25 age group again makes up a majority of victims of assaults between 2002/2003 and 2004/2005, and while the number of victims has declined each year the percentage of young people being targeted has varied from 53% in 2002/2003 to 48% the following year and 50% in 2004/2005. Overall young people under the age of 25 were the victims in 58% of paramilitary 'punishment' shootings over this period and were victims of 50% of beatings.

Table 23. Casualties of Paramilitary Style assaults

	2002/2003		2003/2004		2004/2005	
	0-25	All ages	0-25	All ages	0-25	All ages
Northern Ireland	77	144	71	149	58	116
North Belfast	6	11	11	26	10	21
Derry-Londonderry	1	3	6	8	6	6

Source: PSNI, Central Statistics Unit

Another form of punishment is 'exiling' or 'expulsion', where individuals are forced to leave their home neighbourhood, or even leave Northern Ireland completely, under threat of, often further, physical punishment. It is difficult to establish the exact number of young people who have been driven out, but the Maranatha Community estimated the number of exiles in 2002 to be some 3,000 people including dependents (Kennedy 2003).

The high level of paramilitary threats to young people has been highlighted in the 2000 Young Persons' Behaviour and Attitudes Survey, which found that 6% of young people had been threatened at some time

(NISRA 2000). The same survey in 2003 found that 38% of young people were worried about being threatened by paramilitaries (NISRA 2003). The 2004 Young Life and Times Survey found that 2% of young people had been a victim of a paramilitary beating and 16% of young people had a member of their family or a close friend who had been injured in a paramilitary beating (ARK 2004). Furthermore, nearly 10% of young people had been threatened by a paramilitary group, while more than one quarter (28%) had a member of their family or a close friend who had been threatened by a paramilitary group. The survey concluded that 3% of young people had been forced to leave their home as a result of intimidation, with a further 16% indicating that a member of their family or a close friend had also been forced to move because of intimidation. Paramilitary shootings, beatings, threats and exiling have thus persisted as recurrent activities over recent years.

In all of the areas researched, the paramilitaries were reported to have carried out shootings and beatings and the young people were aware of the role they played in both communities. On several occasions young Catholics made reference to 'the Provies' carrying out shootings and beatings without wearing any mask of disguise so that their face was visible and the individual could be identified. However, even if the individuals did wear a mask this did not stop them from being recognised and, according to two of the young men, it was often possible to guess their identity. Many of the young people said that this was because they wanted to be recognised as the 'police':

They actually think they are local peelers like (Catholic male)

However one young person added that they were only:

Gangsters, that's all they are ... only because they got f—king weapons (Catholic male).

The fear instilled by paramilitaries was largely a result of the fact that they had weapons and were willing to use them. In Galliagh in early 2003 the INLA issued a statement regarding anti-social behaviour in the area. They announced that they would be organising patrols to *'empower and establish confidence within the community'*. According to the local press, these patrols involved masked and armed members patrolling the area and firing a volley of shots before departing (*Derry News* 30 January 2003). Two of the young males interviewed commented on these events, which did not appear to impact on them unduly:

The INLA went mad one time ... last week ... they made an announcement, that if all drug dealers, if they didn't stop on Monday, some certain time, they were all getting shot ... it didn't stop ... it is like it never gonna stop (Catholic male).

A 21-year old male said that neither the INLA nor the IRA were respected within the community and that people only had 'fear' for them. He emphasised that *'nobody wants to get shot'* and that he would rather *'be lifted by the cops'*. Other young people expressed similar views. The young people were aware of the procedure for carrying out punishment shootings and beatings, which tended to involve one or two warnings, and after that you were either beaten or shot. However, young people said that sometimes no warning was given and the attack appeared to be more of a case of random violence. One young male from Galliagh referred to this approach as *'pick and mix'* where young people were simply picked upon and if a group of young people were standing about the paramilitaries arrived, and *'whoever is there gets it'*. Another young man spoke of his experiences with the paramilitaries in the area and commented on how he had been scared by the experience:

They chase us all the time ... they patrol the area ... in Galliagh mostly ... there are about thirty of them ... they are all older, they don't tell you nothing, they don't even talk to you or anything ... it is scary enough (Catholic male).

Discussions with young people about the paramilitary groups centred very much on their role in 'punishments', which were felt to be often conducted unfairly and without any justification. It also emerged that in some cases the young people would be told to leave the area. One young male referred to a sixteen-year-old friend who had been *'chucked out of the area'*. He received a warning from the INLA after being caught stealing and had been told to leave and was now living on the Isle of Man. A 21-year old male said that he had heard of numerous incidents where young people had been *'told to leave'* the area.

In the White City estate, the young people were also aware of the presence of the paramilitaries. They noted that young people were often told to *'move on'* or to stop doing what they were doing. A 12-year old male said that they would give warnings but if you kept on carrying out the actions you were punished – even at his age,

They would come up and say 'right out, I don't want to see yous anywhere near this corner' but then we have nowhere to go or to stand in the middle of the street (Protestant male).

Researcher - Do they threaten you?

No...they give you warnings

Researcher - What about shootings and beatings?

Yes, even our age.

In some cases the young people were told to turn up at a particular place the following day to help clean the area up. One of the interviewees referred to this as *'community service'*. Many of the adults were also aware of the presence and activities of paramilitary groups and it was generally assumed that warnings would be given if:

Somebody is perceived as stepping out of line (Protestant adult).

In other areas one of the main roles of the paramilitaries was in maintaining a presence in the community and 'keeping an eye' on things:

Paramilitaries are there, have been there and will continue to be in the background, I don't think, and that is not to say that they influence any less (Catholic youthworker).

In the case of Sunningdale, many adults in the area were critical of the paramilitaries, and a majority of respondents (68%) believed that there was no role for the paramilitaries, compared to only 18% who were in favour of their presence. A number of reasons were identified as to why paramilitary groups should not have a role within Sunningdale. The two main reasons indicated by respondents were 'violence is not an option' and 'the area has suffered enough'. A group of young people in the Tiger's Bay area of North Belfast felt that the paramilitaries used physical violence and did not contribute positively to society:

They would just beat you (Protestant male).

When young people in both Derry Londonderry and North Belfast were asked whether these beatings and shootings worked as a form of deterrent, the overall impression was that they did have some influence and they created an atmosphere of fear among young people. In some areas the paramilitary presence was not so strong but it was believed that they still operated in the background even if they did not have an overt physical presence. When the issue of the role played by paramilitaries within their areas was raised, many young people were often reluctant to even enter into any form of discussion. In some cases a previously noisy and talkative group would just go quiet. Acts of rebellion and hostility towards the local paramilitaries have also been identified in previous research (Hall 1999; Todd 2002). Harland (2001) showed that many young men perceived punishment shootings and attacks to be unjustified, but also noted that any form of protest involved extreme risk-taking for the young people.

The surveys in Galliagh and Sunningdale both indicated that there is a very limited level of support for paramilitary groups among the young people. A majority of young people in Sunningdale saw no role for paramilitaries in their community and there were similar findings in Galliagh. However, young people also acknowledged the reality of an ongoing presence of paramilitary groups. The North Belfast survey of young people indicated that a third of young people (34%) felt that the paramilitary groups had a degree of authority in their area, a figure that was only superseded by the police, which 39% of respondents identified as the main authority (Byrne, Conway and Ostermeyer 2005). However, the same survey indicated that only 12% of young people said they would choose to contact the paramilitaries if they were attacked and 37% said that the police should give greater priority to dealing with paramilitary activity in the area.

Defending the Area

Although the young people were hostile towards the paramilitaries because of the way they were confronted and assaulted, there was also a degree of ambivalence to their general presence. Some were basically hostile to them in any shape or form, with comments like: *I don't like them (paramilitaries)* (Protestant female) and *They give the area a bad name* (Protestant male), but others were more uncertain: *It depends on who they are* (Protestant male). Some of the young people felt that the paramilitaries were necessary to protect the area from outside threat, and thus contributed positively in some ways to a sense of safety and security. However, others felt that they only made things worse and the paramilitaries were in fact responsible for much of the violence at the interfaces and they therefore helped create the sense of insecurity they claimed to be protecting the area from.

Support for paramilitaries thus varied both within each of the areas and between the different areas. Young people in White City viewed the paramilitaries as being *'both good and bad'*; on one hand they were seen to *'defend the area'* but were also *'tough'* when it came to punishments. Support for paramilitaries was evident by the erection of paramilitary flags, mainly the flags of the UDA/UFF, which was seen as an important marker of territory and gave a clear message to the Catholic/nationalist community that they were not welcome. Similarly, the paramilitaries in the Fountain were considered to be standing up against the *'enemy'*, as the area had been under persistent attack and the community in the Fountain therefore needed their help. One young male referred to an incident in 2002 after a World Cup match in which the Republic of Ireland was beaten by Spain. People in the Fountain waved Union Jacks to celebrate the defeat, but this resulted in an attack on the area by a large group of men wearing Celtic and Republic of Ireland shirts and which in turn led to hand to hand fighting in the street. One male described the incident:

There was around a thousand trying to invade the Fountain ... and there were 200 of the Derry Battalion of the UDA over and helped and saved the place I would have said (Protestant male).

In his view the UDA were therefore needed to protect and safeguard the area from the possibility of future attacks. A young male from the Bogside who was involved in the perceived 'attack', acknowledged the role of loyalist paramilitaries:

They were all over from the Waterside ... a big crowd of them and a big crowd of Catholics (Catholic male).

But, perhaps surprisingly, he felt that this was *'good'* as it only increased the excitement of the fighting. This again emphasises the *'buzz'* that some young people receive from participating in different forms of collective violence.

For some of the young men the paramilitary presence was a necessary fact of life, and the paramilitaries were not seen as *'scary'*, but rather could provide some reassurance:

The loyalist paramilitaries you know most of them like and they are helpful, a bit more helpful than the police (Protestant male).

This perhaps throws the focus on the fact that for many of the young people the members of paramilitary organisations are not anonymous, hooded, unknown individuals but actually were adult members of their local community. They were people who were seen and known in a variety of settings and activities and, while in some circumstances the paramilitaries offered a threat to some people, to others they provided some sense of reassurance.

The fragmented sectarian geography of North Belfast was also reflected in the power or control that different groups exercised in different areas, this is particularly the case in Protestant areas where tensions existed between Mount Vernon, which has a predominant UVF presence, and neighbouring Shore Road, which is a predominately UDA area. The area in which young people lived thus had an impact on how they identified with a particular grouping. It was also clear that in North Belfast the various feuds among loyalist paramilitary groups had an impact on the relationships between people in various areas, even though to an outsider each of the communities was Protestant.

Various reasons for joining paramilitary groups were discussed by some of the young people. In some cases young people actively chose to join an organisation, although the choice of which particular organisation they might join would be dictated by such factors as family background and areas of residence, while for others coercion was a more significant factor in joining an organisation. For some there appeared to be little question of whether they should join, rather it was a practical necessity:

For safety and protection I guess (Protestant male).

Many of the young people could not really see the point of joining a paramilitary grouping:

Some people might … most people won't. Things are changing, in a few years time I don't think they will be around as much (Catholic male).

A similar view was held by other young people, who felt that the control held by paramilitary groups would make joining difficult:

Why join some boys that have threatened you or something, or given you a beating or given some of your mates a beating? (Catholic male).

However, others said that many were forced to join as a result of peer-pressure. In Tiger's Bay, for example, some young people referred to the paramilitaries offering a limited range of alternatives to a beating or shooting, which might include joining the organisation. Even so some young people did not consider joining to be the better option:

You are offered the choice of either joining or being beaten ... I would take a beating any time (Protestant male).

It was however difficult to follow this up as the issue of the recruitment of young people into paramilitary organisations and their involvement in paramilitary activities was a sensitive issue. This difficulty has been noted by others who have tried to research this area. Smyth and Campbell (2005) refer to the somewhat ambivalent attitude among paramilitary organisations in relation to recruitment of new members, and in particular to the recruitment of young people, particularly for those groups which claim to be on ceasefire. In some of the areas young people would refer to other paramilitary groupings, such as Real IRA and Continuity IRA, being active in Catholic areas, but were reluctant to discuss the issue further. In the various discussions with young people it was difficult to establish how far they might be formally involved in paramilitary activity. The everlasting impression was that in many cases the young men were less involved in organised violence but rather were mainly involved in the less organised street violence and disorder at the interfaces.

Controlling interface violence

There seemed to be a degree of confusion among many of the young people about the role played by the paramilitaries in relation to the various outbreaks of interface violence. Some young people felt that they actively encouraged interface violence and the involvement of young people in such violence, whereas others said they did not. However, this may be more a reflection of the diverse and varied roles that members of the different paramilitary groups played at different times or in different areas. In Tiger's Bay and the New Lodge, interviewees felt that the paramilitaries did not encourage violence but rather worked to stop it. Young people in both areas felt that in recent times the paramilitaries had 'moved in' as tension rose and prevented the violence. One of the young males in New Lodge said:

They [the Provies] would slap the head of you or something. (Catholic male)
or
They would tell you to move back (Catholic male).

Similar views were expressed in Newington, where 'Provies':

Used to come down and try to stop you like ... most of the times they did stop you (Catholic male).

Loyalist paramilitaries were also seen to be discouraging violence. On the Limestone Road the presence of the CCTV cameras was acknowledged as helping to reduce violence but the young people also believed that the UDA had contributed to the reduction of disorder. They also noted that the UDA were reported to have punished young people who started riots along the interface. In Tiger's Bay one young male said that young people who started riots were likely to be punished by local paramilitaries.

However, in other locations some young people claimed to have been actively encouraged by paramilitaries to help start violence, or not to have been actively discouraged. In Whitewell and White City the local paramilitaries were seen to be contributing towards the violence around the interfaces, although their attitudes to violence could be inconsistent. One female said:

They try to tell you to get back but sometimes they stand back and tell you to go up (Catholic female)

This contradictory approach was echoed by young people in a number of other areas, where sometimes the young people had initiated fighting or violence on the interface but on other occasions had been told off by paramilitaries:

They would also tell us to go away (Protestant male)
or
They would just tell you to watch yourself (Protestant male).

The young people who were involved with this research had a diverse range of experiences with paramilitary organisations, and this in turn had led to a varied range of attitudes towards these bodies. While in general the young people were hostile to the continued presence of paramilitary groups in their communities, they did also recognise the pragmatics of the current situation, and some young people acknowledged that the paramilitary groups did play a positive role at times in providing a degree of safety and security both from threats from outside and from some elements within their communities. However, the young people were also aware of being manipulated at times when they were encouraged to engage in rioting, only to later be criticised for such behaviour. Although many young people were generally critical of the role of other structures of authority in their communities, such as the police, the potential for the paramilitaries to use violence to impose their authority was a factor that inexorably coloured many people's views and meant that the paramilitary organisations were ultimately viewed through a lens of fear.

Restorative Justice

One attempt to respond to the role of young people in forms of crime and anti-social behaviour, while keeping them out of the criminal justice system and away from the violent 'punishments' imposed by the paramilitaries, has been through the creation of various restorative justice programmes. The primary focus of restorative justice, compared with the established retributive justice system, is to respond to the disruption of social relationships caused by anti-social behaviour and attempt to heal and rebuild the relationships rather than using the law to exact punishment (Knox and Monaghan 2003; McEvoy and Newburn 2003). In Northern Ireland the initial work in developing models of restorative justice was taken within the community realm and among ex-prisoners organisations (Auld et al 1999; Winston 1997) but the police and other statutory agencies have also adopted restorative approaches.

There are two main restorative justice projects, the loyalist Alternatives project and the republican Community Restorative Justice (CRJ) project. Both projects involve mediating between paramilitary groups and (predominately) young people under threat from shootings and beatings, but they also take referrals from community and statutory agencies. In the Alternatives programme each individual is allocated a personal caseworker who works with the perpetrator to make amends to the victim. The process may also involve forms of community reparation and identifying ways of self-improvement. CRJ deals with issues of assault, intimidation, bullying and abuse, neighbourhood conflict, intra-family conflict and youth at serious risk in the community. Alternatives, in contrast to CRJ, also work closely with the statutory justice agencies, including the police.

CRJ is established in three areas of Derry Londonderry: Creggan (Smyth, Hamilton and Thomson 2002), Bogside-Brandywell and Shantallow and has also extended its programme to the city centre. In each area CRJ has tried to prevent young people from getting involved in trouble. For example, in the Bogside CRJ has been involved trying to prevent attacks on the Fountain and in the city centre they have tried to prevent street fights and disturbances. CRJ has yet to be established in the Galliagh area, but has been in place for a number of years in Greater Shantallow, as part of CRJ North West.

Some of the young people in Galliagh were sceptical about restorative justice, in particular because of the close connections between CRJ and the wider republican movement through the involvement of prominent ex-prisoners. For example, one 21-year old male stated that he found it difficult to distinguish between CRJ and paramilitaries, which seemed to be two facets of the same organisation:

If you shoot them and beat them and that doesn't work, I cannot see how sitting down talking to them would work. (Catholic male)

One example of CRJ's role in dealing with problems occurred when the residents of Galliagh Park contacted a local councillor after they experienced problems with young people drinking and making noise in the street and joy-riding at weekends. The councillor, together with local residents, CRJ and Off the Streets Community Youth Initiative, met with the young people to talk about the problems from the residents' perspectives. As a result they were able to bring about a solution, the young people tended not to congregate in the same area and no further complaints were received. This also meant a dialogue had been established between the residents and the groups of young people, which could be used to ensure problems did not arise in the future.

Many of the young people were critical of the restorative justice ethos. In part the young people's views seemed to be due to their limited knowledge of the restorative approach, philosophy and process. Instead their understanding of restorative justice focused on the role of republicans in the project and the fact that young people who had been creating trouble might receive favourable treatment through this programme. In some ways this was similar to the concerns expressed about youth workers offering trips and special programmes to young people who were engaged in disruptive behaviour.

In North Belfast the Alternatives programme works with young people and attempts to involve them in a variety of activities that benefit both the young people and the local community. These include working individually with young people as part of the referral programme, or with larger groups, arranging activities for young people in the area, involving them in programmes like the Duke of Edinburgh's Scheme. In Sunningdale, North Belfast Alternatives were involved in establishing programmes with young people who had been referred from the local school. The young people in Sunningdale were more positive about Alternatives than young people in Galliagh were about CRJ. This appeared to be because the young people felt that through Alternatives they were involved in productive activities and were given constructive things to do.

The various community-based restorative justice programmes have had a limited impact in the areas that were researched. In some areas the projects were only just being established, in others they were still to be established. They therefore had had little impact on the lives of the young people involved in the research. Nevertheless, many of the young people had categorised the idea of restorative justice as either another attempt by the broader republican and loyalist movements to exert authority over them, or as a soft option that would keep troublemakers from both the criminal justice system and from the more violent justice of the paramilitaries. There was thus a degree of scepticism and cynicism about the potential benefits to young people of community based restorative justice programmes.

Summary

This section has considered some of the relationships between young people living in interface communities and the main structures of adult authority that they engage with in the broad public arena. This found that in general the relations between young people and the police and between young people and the paramilitary structures were not based on any sense of respect and trust, but rather on hostility and fear and were underpinned by a threat of violence. Many of the young people seemed to accept that their reality was a life in which forms of threat and violence were a norm. They might expect to be verbally harassed and chased by the police, and on occasion they might be physically assaulted if they were caught. Equally they lived with the threat of physical violence or intimidation from the local paramilitaries if they crossed certain boundaries of acceptable behaviour.

The problem for many young people was that they were not sure what the boundaries were, or that the boundaries of acceptable behaviour might be changed. While most of the young people acknowledged that at times they did participate in a variety of forms of what has been broadly classified as anti-social behaviour, they also felt that too often they were too readily classified as trouble makers and too readily targeted as a source of local problems. For many of the young people much of what they did was similar to what the adult generation had done in previous years. Overall there was a sense of mutual suspicion and distrust between the young people and many of the adults who seek to impose a sense of order over public space or to impose their authority over the local communities. As has been noted throughout this report these mutually suspicious and mistrustful relationships are sustained not only by a lack of constructive dialogue, but also by the legacy of violence that legitimises and condones the use of force too readily and in too many contexts.

7. Conclusions

The findings from this research project hopefully provide a comprehensive account of young people's experiences and perceptions of violence, community conflict and disorder in a number of areas of Belfast and Derry Londonderry. The violence and disorder at interfaces are well researched and it is evident that young people actively participate in a variety of forms of violence, which may be initiated both by themselves and by adults. Young people often saw themselves as being in the forefront of this violence, which they acknowledged was often 'recreational' rather than in any way politically motivated. However, it is also important to note the different range of experiences of categories of violence in different areas, among different communities and also among young people of different ages and gender. The prominence of violent assaults in Derry city centre was often referred to, whereas young people in Belfast raised few concerns about safety in their city centre.

The combination of recurrent violence and a lack of any wider social engagement appear to be both a cause and effect of a sense of alienation among a significant number of young people. Many of those living in interface areas have a very negative outlook on life. Their attitudes have been shaped by experiences of persistent sectarian and communal violence and many young people continue to experience intimidation and violence as a part of their daily lives. Although some young people are willing to engage in cross-community activities, there is also a significant minority who show no desire of being more involved with the neighbouring community. Some even advocate greater segregation and are readily involved in sectarian and violent behaviour.

It was however striking that some young people retained an optimistic view towards cross-community work, but in many interface areas this work was particularly difficult and challenging. Even in areas where interface violence had been effectively stopped, the relationships between the two communities remained strained, with limited levels of interaction and co-operation between the young people. There was a preference towards engaging with young people from the other community who lived away from the immediate area, and many young people and youth leaders felt this type of approach worked best. Many young people in fact expressed an unease about *'crossing over'* to use facilities and amenities perceived to be *'on the other side'* and the difficulties of accessing ostensibly shared resources because of their religious background.

Young people are involved in various forms of anti-social behaviour, ranging from graffiti and vandalism to physical assaults. One recurrent theme in this context was underage drinking and the ease with which alcohol was available to young people. In this context it was also worth noting that young people are not a homogenous entity and some went to great pains to dissociate themselves from groups that they labelled as 'hoods' or 'gluesniffers'. The lower levels of interface violence, particularly in North Belfast, have led to a perceived increase in anti-social behaviour and there were claims that young people had shifted their attention away from activities located at sectarian interfaces to disruptive activities within the residential community.

There is thus a strained relationship in many communities between young people and the main forms of authority and order and in particular where young people feel they are picked upon both by paramilitaries and the police. In almost all of the areas that were researched there was a paramilitary presence, which was often manifest through threats, intimidation and beatings. This also led to a strong anti-paramilitary sentiment among some young people. However, in some areas paramilitary affiliation was a source of identification and young people saw the paramilitary groups as defenders of the areas from outside threat.

Young people from both main communities seem to be alienated from the police in particular. The majority of young people's experiences of contact with the police were, regardless of community background, negative. Young people tended to view the police as unfair and confrontational and it is thus worth noting that attacking the police was seen as a legitimate activity. Few of the young people we spoke with referred to any interaction with the police outside of their involvement in violence or in anti-social behaviour. It was, however, difficult to obtain any ideas as to how this situation might be improved from young people, for many this poor relationship seemed to be regarded as inevitable.

Herein lies a challenge for the communities and statutory agencies alike. Some of the solutions that are currently being applied, such as telling young people to move on or asking the paramilitary groups to deal with the problem, are hardly solutions. Similarly, the introduction of ASBOs could lead to further alienation of some young people, particularly as few appeared to be aware of what an ASBO involves. The challenges increasingly appear to be to work on the intra-community dimensions and try to improve young people's relationships within their communities. Although it has become something of a stock response to complain about a lack of facilities, it is still incumbent on adults and local organisations to engage more effectively with young people and to develop a more detailed approach to address their needs. The findings from the research showed that the needs and concerns of young people were similar throughout the areas and work is ongoing in many areas to involve young people in the design as well as the implementation of programmes and activities both through statutory agencies and voluntary groups. The intensity and energy that young people are prepared to commit towards some 'cultural activities' highlight the possibilities of a commitment and a valuable resource, which needs to be developed. What also comes across strongly from this research is that there is no single solution to the multitude of issues relating to violence and disorder involving young people. Rather, as has been noted by numerous other pieces of work, what is needed is a multi-agency approach to the issues of youth violence, involving representatives from the voluntary, community and statutory agencies.

References

ARK (2004) *Young Life and Times Survey*. Belfast: ARK, Queen's University.
Belfast Interface Project (1998) *Young People on the Interface*. Belfast: BIP
Boal, F., Neville, J., Douglas, H. and Orr, J. (1982) *Integration and Division: Geographical Perspectives on the Northern Ireland Problem*. London: Academic Press.
Byrne, J. (2005) *Interface Violence in East Belfast during 2002: The Impact on Residents of Short Strand and Inner East Belfast* . Belfast, ICR.
Byrne, J., Conway, M. and Ostermeyer, M. (2005) Young People's Attitudes and Experiences of Policing, Violence and Community Safety in North Belfast. Belfast: Northern Ireland Policing Board
Byrne, J., Hansson, U. and Jarman, N. (2005) Teenage Kicks. *Arvac Bulletin* No 98.
Cadwallader, A. (2004) *Holy Cross: The Untold Story*. Belfast: The Brehon Press Ltd.
Cairns, E. (1996) *Children and Political Violence*. Oxford: Blackwell.
Carling, A., Davies, D., Fernandes-Bakshi, A., Jarman, N. and Nias, P. (2004) *Fair Justice for All? The Response of the Criminal Justice System to the Bradford Disturbances of July 2001*. Bradford: Programme for a Peaceful City.
Cohen, S. (2002) *Folk Devils and Moral Panics: Third Edition*. London: Routledge.
Connolly, P. and Maginn, P. (1999) *Sectarianism, Children and Community Relations in Northern Ireland*. Coleraine: Centre for the Study of Conflict, University of Ulster.
Conway, M. and Hansson. U. (2005) *Young Women's Attitudes and Experiences of Violence and Community Safety in the Greater New Lodge Area*. Belfast: ICR (Unpublished)
Corrigan, S. (1998) *Caught in the Middle*. Belfast: Northern Ireland Women's Aid.
Doherty, E. and McCormack, J. (2003) *Underage Drinking in the Derry City Council Area. Research undertaken on behalf of the Foyle Underage Drinking Steering Group*. Derry: Derry Healthy Cities.
Eitle, D. and Turner, R. (2002) Exposure to Community Violence and Young Adult Crime: The Effects of Witnessing Violence, Traumatic Victimization, and Other Stressful Life Events. *Journal of Research in Crime and Delinquency* 39 (2): 214-237.
Ellison, G. (2001) *Young People, Crime, Policing and Victimisation in Northern Ireland*. Belfast: Institute of Criminology, Queens University.
Fay, M-T., Morrissey, M., Smyth, M. and Wong, T. (1997) *Mapping Troubles Related Deaths in Northern Ireland*. Derry Londonderry: INCORE.

Fay, M-T., Morrissey, M. and Smyth, M. (1999a) *Northern Ireland's Troubles: The Human Costs.* London: Pluto Press.

Fay, M-T., Morrissey, M., Smyth, M. and Wong, T. (1999b) *The Cost of the Troubles Study. Report on the Northern Ireland Survey: the experience and impact of the Troubles.* Derry Londonderry: INCORE.

Gill, M. and Spriggs, A. (2005) *Assessing the Impact of CCTV.* Home Office Research Study 292. London: Home Office.

Hall, M (1999) *Young People Speak Out. Newhill Youth Development Team.* Newtonabbey: Island Publications

Hall, M. (2002) *Reuniting the Shankill. A report on the Greater Shankill Community Exhibition and Convention.* Belfast: Farset Community Think Thank

Hamilton, J., Radford, K. and Jarman, N. (2003) *Policing Accountability and Young People.* Belfast: ICR.

Hamilton, J., Radford, K. and Jarman, N. (2004) 'Learning to Listen' – Young people and the Police in Northern Ireland. *Youth And Policy* No 84: 5-20.

Harland, K. (2001) The Challenges and Potential of Developing a more Effective Youth Work Curriculum with Young Men. *Child Care in Practice*, 7 (4), 288-300.

Health Promotion Agency (2002), *Attitudes and behaviour of young adult drinkers in Northern Ireland. A qualitative study.* Belfast: Health Promotion Agency for Northern Ireland.

Jarman, N. (1997) *On the Edge: Community Perspectives on the Civil Disturbances in North Belfast, June–September 1996.* Belfast: Community Development Centre.

Jarman, N. (2002), *Managing Disorder. Responding to Interface Violence in North Belfast.* Belfast: Office of the First Minister and Deputy First Minister

Jarman, N. (2004) From War to Peace? Changing Patterns of Violence in Northern Ireland 1990-2003. *Terrorism and Political Violence,* 16 (3), 420-438.

Jarman, N. (2005) Teenage Kicks: Young Women and their Involvement in Violence and Disorderly Behaviour. *Child Care in Practice* 11 (3), 341-356.

Jarman, N. and O'Halloran, C. (2000) *Peacelines or Battlefields: Responding to violence in Interface Areas.* Belfast: Community Development Centre

Jarman, N. and O'Halloran, C. (2001) 'Recreational Rioting: Young People, interface areas and violence.' *Child Care in Practice,* 7 (1), 2-16.

Kelly, B. (2002) Young People's Views on Communities and Sectarianism in Northern Ireland. *Child Care in Practice* 8 (1), 65-72

Kennedy, L. (2003) *They shoot children, don't they?* Third and final report. A report Prepared for the Northern Ireland Committee against Terror.

Knox, C. and Monaghan, R. (2003) 'Fear of Reprisal', in Lee, R. and Stanko, E. (eds) *Researching Violence,* London: Routledge.

McEvoy, K. and Newburn, T. (eds) (2003) *Criminology, Conflict Resolution and Restorative Justice.* Basingstoke: Palgrave.

McEvoy-Levy, S. (2001) *Youth as Social and Political Agents: Issues in post-Settlement Peace Building. Paper prepared for the Fifth International Conference of the Ethnic Studies Network.* Derry Londonderry: INCORE.

McGrellis, S. (2004) *Pushing the Boundaries in Northern Ireland: Young People, Violence and Sectarianism. Families and Social Capital ESRC Research Group.* London: London South Bank University.

McVeigh, R. (1994) *Harassment: 'Its Part of Life Here'.* Belfast: Committee on the Administration of Justice.

Miller, L., Wasserman, G., Neugebauer, R., Gorman-Smith, G. and Kamboukos, D. (1999) 'Witnessed Community Violence and Antisocial Behaviour in High-Risk Urban Boys'. *Journal of Clinical Child Psychology* No. 28, 2-11.

Mourlon, F. and Hansson, U. (2005) *Crime, A waste of time? Crime and anti-social behaviour in Sunningdale. A collaboration between young people in Sunningdale, North Belfast Alternatives, LINC and ICR.* Belfast: Institute for Conflict Research.

Nagle, J. (2004) *'Up the Hoods': the Discursive Formation of Belfast Youth as Frankenstein's Monster, Urban Guerrilla and Folk Devil.* Unpublished paper.

NIACRO (2001) *Galliagh Community Safety Survey.* Belfast: NIACRO.

North Belfast Community Action Unit (2002) *Report of the Project Team:* May 2002. Belfast: Office of the First Minister and Deputy First Minister.

North Belfast Community Action Unit (2004) *Evaluation of the Youth Development Programme 2002-2003.* Belfast: Deloitte & Touche.

Northern Ireland Association for the Care and Resettlement of Offenders (2001) *Ballysillan Community Audit.* Belfast: NIACRO.

Northern Ireland Housing Executive (1999) *Towards a Community Relations Strategy.* Belfast: Northern Ireland Housing Executive.

Northern Ireland Policing Board (2004) *District Policing Partnership DPP Public Consultation Survey, June 2003.* Belfast: Northern Ireland Policing Board.

Northern Ireland Statistics and Research Agency (2000) *Young Persons Behaviour and Attitudes Survey.* Belfast: NISRA.

Northern Ireland Statistics and Research Agency (2001), *Northern Ireland Census.* Belfast: NISRA.

Northern Ireland Statistics and Research Agency (2002) *Young Persons Behaviour and Attitudes Survey.* Belfast: NISRA.

Northern Ireland Statistics and Research Agency (2003) *Young Persons Behaviour and Attitudes Survey.* Belfast: NISRA.

Off the Streets, St Brigid's College and Institute for Conflict Research (2004) *Young People in the Greater Shantallow Area.* Derry: Off the Streets.

Poole, C. and Doherty, M. (1996) *Ethnic Residential Segregation in Northern Ireland.* Coleraine: Centre for the Study of Conflict.

Radical (2002) *Blotting it out: Perceptions and Patterns of Drug Misuse in Four Communities in North Belfast. An Explanatory Needs Analysis*. Belfast: RADICAL.

Reilly, J., Muldoon, O. and Byrne, C. (2004) Young Men as Victims and Perpetrators of Violence in Northern Ireland: A Qualitative Analysis. *Journal of Social Issues*, 60 (3), 469-484.

Scarpa, A. (2001) Community Violence Exposure in a Young Adult Sample: Lifetime Prevalence and Socioemotional Effects. *Journal of Consulting and Clinical Psychology* No. 46, 932-46.

Smyth, M. (1998) *Half the Battle; Understanding the effects of the 'Troubles' on children and young people in Northern Ireland*. Derry Londonderry: INCORE.

Smyth, M. and Campbell, P. (2005) *Young People and Armed Violence in Northern Ireland*. Rio de Janeiro, Viva Rio.

Smyth, M. and Scott, M. (2000), *The Youthquest 2000 Survey. A report on young people's views and experiences in Northern Ireland*. Derry Londonderry: INCORE.

Smyth, M., Hamilton, J. and Thomson, K (2002) *Creggan Community Restorative Justice: An Evaluation and Suggested Way Forward*. Belfast: ICR.

Smyth, P. (2001) From Subject to Citizen? The Role of Youth Work in the Building of Democracy in Northern Ireland: a personal view in Working with Children and Young People in Violently Divided Societies. *Papers from South Africa and Northern Ireland*. Edited by Smyth, M and Thompson, K.

Todd, H. (2002) *Young People in the Short Strand Speak Out*. Belfast: University of Ulster

Triax Taskforce (2003) *Tackling Inequalities – Bridging the Gap. Triax Consultation Report*. Derry Londonderry: Triax Taskforce.

University of Ulster (2003) *R City Centre 2. An analysis of the Mapping Exercise and the Views of Young People on Belfast City Centre and its Youth services*. Belfast: University of Ulster.

Welsh, B. and Farrington, D. (2002) *Crime Prevention Effects of Closed Circuit Television: A Systematic Review*. Home Office Research Study 252. London: Home Office.

Winston, T. (1997) Alternatives to Punishment Beatings and Shootings in a Loyalist Community in Belfast. *Critical Criminology*, 8 (1): 122-128.

Woodvale Resource Centre (1998), *Report on Ardoyne-Springfield Interface*. Belfast: Woodvale Resource Centre.

Youth Council for Northern Ireland (2000) *Taking the Initiative. Promoting Young People's Involvement in Decision Making in Northern Ireland*. Belfast: Youth Council for Northern Ireland.

Zurawski, N. (2005) "I Know Where You Live!" – Aspects of Watching, Surveillance and Social Control in a Conflict Zone. *Surveillance and Society* 2(4) www.surveillance-and-society.org

ICR REPORTS

The following is a list of the most recent research reports that have been produced by ICR. Wherever possible reports are made available on our website, some however remain the property of the commissioning body and are retained as internal documents. A full list of reports, papers and articles can be found on our website.

Interface Violence in East Belfast during 2002: The impact on residents of Short Strand and Inner East Belfast. Jonny Byrne, (2005) Funded by EU Programme for Peace and Reconciliation.

Interface Issues: An Annotated Bibliography. Mary Conway and Jonny Byrne, (2005) Commissioned by Belfast Interface Project.

New Migrant Communities in East Tyrone. Jennifer Betts and Jennifer Hamilton, (2005) Commissioned by East Tyrone College of Further and Higher Education.

No Longer a Problem? Sectarian Violence in Northern Ireland. Neil Jarman, (2005) Commissioned by Office of the First Minister and Deputy First Minister.

Ballysillan Residents' Attitudes towards Church Participation, Community Involvement and Neighbourhood Safety. Mary Conway, (2005). Ballysillan Bridgebuilding Forum and ICR.

Young People's Attitudes and Experiences of Policing, Violence and Community Safety in North Belfast. Jonny Byrne, Mary Conway and Malcolm Ostermeyer, (2005). Commissioned by the Northern Ireland Policing Board.

Young People in Community Conflict. Jonny Byrne, Jennifer Hamilton and Ulf Hansson, (2005). Commissioned by Northern Health and Social Services Board.

Sectarian and Racist Chill Factors in Armagh College. Jennifer Hamilton, (2005). Commissioned by Armagh College of Further and Higher Education.

Community Cohesion: Applying Learning from Groundwork in Northern Ireland. Neil Jarman, Libby Keyes, Jenny Pearce and Derick Wilson, (2004) Commissioned by Groundwork UK.

Sectarianism in Armagh City and District Council Area. Jennifer Hamilton, (2004) Commissioned by Community Relations Council.

Out of Sight: Young People and Paramilitary Exiling in Northern Ireland. Jonny Byrne, (2004). Commissioned by Save the Children and NIACRO.

Report on the Consultation about proposals for a Chinese Community Centre on Donegall Pass, Belfast. Neil Jarman, (2004). Commissioned by Belfast City Council.

Community Relations, Community Cohesion and Regeneration: A training and development strategy for Groundwork Northern Ireland. Neil Jarman and Paul Hutchinson, (2004). Commissioned by Groundwork NI.

Young People in the Greater Shantallow Area. Ulf Hansson, (2004). Off the Streets and ICR.

Sectarianism in the Limavady Borough Council Area. Jonny Byrne, (2004). Commissioned by Community Relations Council.

Mediation Northern Ireland Policing Project: Interim Evaluation. Neil Jarman, (2004). Commissioned by Mediation Northern Ireland.

Demography, Development and Disorder: Changing Patterns of Interface Areas. Neil Jarman, (2004). Commissioned by Community Relations Council.

Crime–A Waste of Time. Crime and Anti-Social Behaviour in Sunningdale. Fabrice Mourlon and Ulf Hansson, (2004). North Belfast Alternatives and ICR.

Evaluation Report of Diversity Challenges. Ruth Moore, Brandon Hamber and Neil Jarman, (2004). Commissioned by Diversity Challenges.

Sectarianism in the Antrim Borough Council Area. Jonny Byrne, (2004). Commissioned by Community Relations Council.

Sectarianism in the Larne District Council Area. Jonny Byrne, (2004). Commissioned by Community Relations Council.

Legislative Provisions for Hate Crime across EU Member States. Rebecca Thomas, (2004). ICR.

Migrant Workers in Northern Ireland. Kathryn Bell, Neil Jarman and Thomas Lefebvre, (2004). Commissioned by the Office of the First Minister and Deputy First Minister.

Racist Harassment in Northern Ireland. Neil Jarman and Rachel Monaghan, (2004). Commissioned by the Office of the First Minister and Deputy First Minister.

Young People's Attitudes and Experiences of Sectarianism and Community Conflict in Larne. Jonny Byrne, (2004). Commissioned by YMCA.

The Impact of Political Conflict on Children in Northern Ireland. Marie Smyth with Marie Therese Fay, Emily Brough and Jennifer Hamilton, (2004). ICR.

A Review of the Health and Social Care Needs of Victims/Survivors of the Northern Ireland Conflict. Jennifer Hamilton, Jonny Byrne and Neil Jarman, (2003). Commissioned by Eastern Health and Social Services Board.

An Acceptable Prejudice? Homophobic Violence and Harassment in Northern Ireland. Neil Jarman and Alex Tennant, (2003). Commissioned by the Office of the First Minister and Deputy First Minister.

Young People and Politics. North Belfast Community Research Group, (2003). LINC Resource Centre and ICR.

Policing, Accountability and Young People. Jennifer Hamilton, Katy Radford and Neil Jarman, (2003). Commissioned by Office of the Police Ombudsman for Northern Ireland and Northern Ireland Policing Board.

Analysis of Incidents of Racial Harassment Recorded by the Police in Northern Ireland. Neil Jarman and Rachel Monaghan, (2003). Commissioned by the Office of the First Minister and Deputy First Minister.

Human Rights and Community Relations: Competing or Complimentary Approaches in Response to Conflict? Neil Jarman (ed), (2002). ICR.

The Human Impact of the Troubles on Housing Provision and Policy. Jennifer Hamilton, Rachel Monaghan and Marie Smyth, (2002). Commissioned by Northern Ireland Housing Executive.

Creggan Community Restorative Justice: An Evaluation and Suggested Way Forward. Marie Smyth, Jennifer Hamilton and Kirsten Thomson, (2002). ICR and St Columb's Park House.

Caring Through the Troubles: Health and Social Services in North and West Belfast. Marie Smyth, Mike Morrissey and Jennifer Hamilton, (2001). Commissioned by North and West Health and Social Services Board.

Reviewing REAL Provision: An Evaluation of Provision and Support for People Affected by the Northern Ireland Troubles. Jennifer Hamilton, Kirsten Thomson and Marie Smyth, (2001). Commissioned by Northern Ireland Voluntary Trust.